THE GEOGRAPHY OF HEAVEN

THE GEOGRAPHY OF HEAVEN

BY MARK JOHANSEN

Electric Tactics

Monroe, Michigan

CONTENTS

If I have told you earthly things and you do not believe, how will you believe if I tell you heavenly things?

John 3:12

DETAILED CONTENTS

1. The Popular View

What are Heaven and Hell like?

If you asked the average American on the street, you'd probably get an answer something like this:

When a really bad person dies – a murderer or a rapist or a lawyer – they go to Hell. (Well, they probably wouldn't include the lawyer.) (Well, maybe they would.) People who are basically good and decent go to Heaven.

Heaven is a place of sky and clouds. Somewhere in there there's also a city with streets of gold and pearly gates. Saint Peter sits at the pearly gates deciding who will be admitted to Heaven and who will be sent to Hell. He has a big book that tells everything you've done in your life. If you haven't done anything really bad – or some would say, if your good deeds outweigh your bad deeds – he lets you into Heaven. Otherwise you are sent to Hell.

Those who go to Heaven become angels. They wear white robes and have wings and golden halos above their heads. They spend their time floating around the clouds playing harps and singing hymns.

Hell is a place of fire. It is ruled by the Devil, who has red skin, horns and a tail and hooves like a goat, and who carries a pitchfork. Those condemned to Hell spend eternity shoveling coal into the fires.

That's the picture you get from casual, popular descriptions, right? I'm sure we've all seen cartoons of angels flying around clouds and so on.

1.1. Some Problems

And yet ... almost every element of this description is wrong. At least, most of this is not found in the Bible, and what does come from the Bible is badly distorted.

The real Heaven and Hell – the Heaven and Hell described in the Bible – are not cartoons. They are not children's stories. They are not symbols. They are very real places.

Let's take a look at what the Bible actually says about Heaven and Hell.

1.2. The First Problem

Just for starters: Nowhere does the Bible say that anyone goes to Heaven when they die.

But, you might say, doesn't the Bible say something about, "to be absent from the body is to be present with the Lord"? That's right: 2 Corinthians 5:8. It says the saved will be "with the Lord". But it doesn't say that will be in Heaven.

Didn't Jesus assure the thief on the cross, "today you will be with me in Paradise"? Yes he did: Luke 23:43. But he said "in Paradise", not "in Heaven".

Didn't Jesus advise us, "Do not lay up for yourselves treasures on earth ... but lay up for yourselves treasures in Heaven"? Yes, he did: Matthew 6:19-20. But he said that our treasure should be in Heaven, not that we would live there. Most of my earthly treasure is in my 401k retirement plan. But I don't live at the bank. I've never even been to the bank that holds most of my money.

1.3. The Second Problem

The geography of Eternity is far more complicated than most people realize. There are not just two places, Heaven and Hell. There is also "New Earth", "New Jerusalem", "Hades", the "Abyss", etc. Christians generally assume that these are all many different names for just the two places. I think this is a mistake.

In the following chapters, I will go through all the places that the Bible talks about existing in Eternity, and discuss what they are and how they relate to each other.

2. Preliminary Stuff

2.1. Eternity

A side note on terminology: It gets awkward to repeatedly say, "Heaven and Hell and other related places that the Bible talks about". So in this book, I'll refer to these places collectively as "Eternity".

2.2. Sources

How can we know about spiritual things? How can we know about Heaven and Hell?

Ways people try to arrive at the truth about spiritual things include:

- What I'd like to believe
- What most people think
- What the experts say
- What makes logical sense
- What the Bible says

Perhaps stated this way it is obvious how reliable each one is.

"What I'd like to believe": I have often heard people say things like, "I'd like to believe that everyone will go to Heaven", or, "I'd like to believe that God won't allow anything bad to happen to me as long as I'm a good person." One can only say, So what? What you would like to believe has pretty much nothing to do with what is actually true.

You don't hear people say such things about other areas of knowledge. I've never heard someone say, "I'd like to believe that my car will run without gas" or "I'd like to believe that I'll win the lottery." At least, I've never heard anyone say such things with the thought that the fact that these things would be nice to believe in any way makes them true. I'd like to believe that my car will run without gas. But I know that it won't, so I still fill up the tank regularly. Suppose I went to the bank and applied for a big loan, and when they asked how I intended to repay it, I told them, "Well, I'd like to believe that I'll win the lottery." Let's say I don't even mention the fact that I've never bought a lottery ticket. Do you think they'd accept that as collateral? Only in fairy tales do wishes affect reality.

"What most people think": I suppose this is a little better than what you'd like to believe. Maybe if many people think something is true, they have some good reason for thinking that. But maybe not. Maybe most people are wrong. There was a time when "most people" believed that putting leaches on a sick person to suck his blood would help cure disease. I'm sure you've heard many other examples.

"What the experts say": This is a better, but only a little. Presumably experts know what they're talking about. But again, maybe not. If the experts believe something is true because they have solid evidence – scientific experiments or historical documents or whatever sort of evidence is relevant to the question – show me the evidence. Then I'll be convinced by the evidence, and not because the experts said so. If the experts do not have solid evidence, then their idea is no more valuable than that of anyone off the street, or someone who is just throwing out wild speculation. Despite having some credentials as an "expert", if he doesn't have evidence to back up his beliefs, it is just uninformed opinion. Either way, the fact that an expert said so doesn't matter. What matters is the evidence.

"What makes logical sense": Now we are getting to things that have value. A good logical argument based on solid facts has some weight. Mathematicians have built a large body of knowledge based on pure logic. Historians and scientists have built a body of knowledge based on logic applied to raw facts. But of course, there are limits to logic. Human beings make mistakes. Our senses can be fooled. Our thinking can be muddled.

"What the Bible says": When it comes to knowing about spiritual things, the Bible is the ultimate, most reliable source.

Things like Heaven and Hell and angels and demons are outside normal human experience. We can't know about these things by personal experience because we have no way to reach Heaven and Hell. Similarly, we can't know these things through science because we cannot access them at will to perform an experiment.

Suppose you want to know what it is like on the far side of the Moon. Unless you have a few billion dollars handy to start your own space program, there's no way to get there. Only a handful of people and robot space probes have ever been there. The only way to know what it's like is to talk to those people or read their books, or study the pictures and other data sent back by people or robots. (Or get the information from someone who has gotten it from them.)

It's even more difficult to learn about Heaven and Hell. At least in the case of the far side of the Moon, we can make plausible theories based on what we can see on the near side of the Moon. We can work on the assumption that the laws of physics and chemistry there are the same as here on Earth. Etc. But can we say any of that about Heaven and Hell?

If we want to know about Heaven and Hell, we have to turn to someone who was there, to someone who knows. That would be God. Fortunately for us, he wrote a book, and we can read that book.

2.3. Near-Death Experiences

There are people who claim to have died and seen the afterlife and come back. The things they report are called Near Death Experiences, or NDEs. I don't use their accounts in this book, because it is too difficult to know what to make of them, and in the end they don't tell us much. Let me explain.

Jesus told of a man in Hades who asked Abraham that someone be raised from the dead to warn his family:

Luke 16: 27-31 "Then he said, 'I beg you therefore, father, that you would send him to my father's house, for I have five brothers, that he may testify to them, lest they also come to this place of torment.' Abraham said to him, 'They have Moses and the prophets; let them hear them.' And he said, 'No, father Abraham; but if one goes to them from the dead, they will repent.' But he said to him, 'If they do not hear Moses and the prophets, neither will they be persuaded though one rise from the dead.'"

When I first read this story as a young Christian, I found that last statement hard to accept. Surely if someone came back from the dead and told people that he had seen Heaven and Hell with his own eyes, they would believe!

But then stories of NDEs started coming to light. People did, in fact, claim to have died, seen Heaven and Hell, and come back to tell about it. Did this lead all the atheists in the world to cry, "Zounds, we were wrong! Here's eye-witness testimony!" No, it didn't. They simply dismissed these accounts. They said these people were hallucinating, or making the stories up. There are probably some people out there who have been convinced that there is life after death because of such accounts. But I don't think I've ever met such a person. I'm a Christian, and I'm not sure what to make of these stories!

Three things about these stories impress me and make me think they are real:

One: The stories do not match popular ideas about Heaven and Hell.

If these stories were fiction -- whether deliberate lies so they could sell books and get on television, or dreams or delusions -- I'd expect them to generally coincide with popular ideas. I'd think they would talk about seeing angels with white robes and wings and so on, because that's what most people think Heaven is like. A dream or hallucination would be influenced by what you expect to see. Someone lying would likely make their story coincide with what they know their audience expects to hear. But NDEs aren't like this. They typically do not mention angels or harps or Saint Peter. What they do commonly begin with is the person being drawn down a dark tunnel. Before these NDE reports came out, the idea of travelling down a dark tunnel was not part of any popular view of the afterlife. If it's just made up, where did it come from?

Another common element is meeting a "being of light". If a Christian had a hallucination or made up a story, I would expect him to describe simply meeting Christ. I'd expect the Christ of his fantasy to look like the classic pictures: long hair and a beard, wearing a white robe with a blue sash, etc. But that's not what these people report. They report seeing this mysterious being that they think must be Christ.

Two: Despite this, the stories fit the broad outlines of what the Bible says. Their souls leave their bodies. They meet a being who may be Christ. They meet friends and relatives who have died before. There is some sort of review of their lives that may be leading up to judgment. Some report going to a good and happy place and some to a terrible place. Etc.

Three: Many people have reported very similar experiences. This isn't so amazing today now that these stories are "out there" in the popular consciousness, but it was impressive when most of these people had never heard the others' stories.

When someone tells me a story that isn't what I expected to hear, that doesn't match what most people think, but that fits in with other available facts, I am impressed. A hallucination probably wouldn't fit the facts. A deliberate lie would likely be just what the speaker thought I wanted or expected to hear.

Suppose you are on a jury. A witness comes forward who says that the defendant is indeed guilty. But the witness's account of the crime doesn't match the prosecutor's theory of how it was done, nor does it match what all the newspapers are saying happened. But it is consistent with all the physical evidence. I would find that more convincing than someone who backed up the prosecutor 100%. I'd think that if the prosecutor is going to manipulate a witness, he'd have that witness back up everything he said, not give some totally different story.

A clever liar might think through this logic. (Hey, this could be a plot line for a detective novel.) But we're not talking about just one story. We're talking about hundreds of stories. Did all of them think this through? That sounds very unlikely.

And of course, when a number of people who have not talked to each other tell the same story, that's impressive.

But all that said, we're a long way from proof that these stories are true.

It's difficult to study the question scientifically: We can't kill a number of people and then try to bring them back to relate their experiences.

Maybe these are all hallucinations. There may be something about the process of dying that causes a certain type of hallucination. The similarities between the stories may be because these people are all going through a similar process of dying. The explanations I've heard are all very unconvincing and fanciful, but that doesn't prove there isn't a serious explanation out there.

Maybe these people are all making up stories. This would seem to require a huge conspiracy involving thousands of people for no clear motive, but maybe there's something going on that I don't know about.

Maybe the people who write the books and make the TV documentaries are exaggerating the similarities between the stories, and/or "cleaning up" stories to make them sound far more rational and coherent than they really are. Of all attempts to "explain away" NDEs, I'd find that the most plausible, as it requires only a handful of people to be lying or confused.

All that said, even if you accept NDEs as truthful, accurate accounts, they just don't add much to our knowledge of the afterlife. None of the accounts I have read include much concrete information beyond "I went through a dark tunnel, met a being of light who reviewed my life, and met people who had died before me." They'll give details about just what the tunnel was like and who they met, but they don't seem to say much about any events beyond that.

This isn't necessarily surprising. The nature of NDEs is that the person has to be resuscitated for the rest of us to hear the story. So by definition, none of these people were truly, "permanently" dead. Most were clinically dead for just a few minutes. How much could you expect them to see? It's like trying to learn what London is like by talking to someone who flew there, got off the plane, and then at the airport was told that he wouldn't be admitted to the country and had to go back home. All he would know is what he saw of the city from the air and what he saw at the airport. We certainly would have to be very careful about concluding that something *isn't* in London just because he didn't see it. Like the fact that he never met the queen would hardly prove that she doesn't exist. Likewise, some have made much of the fact that people who have had NDEs do not report a final judgment like the Bible says will happen. But presumably God knows that he is going to send them back so their lives aren't over. How could he judge them before their lives are complete? That would be like grading a test before the student has finished taking it.

So this is all I'm going to say about NDEs in this book.

2.4.   Authority of Scripture

For this book I start with the assumption that the Bible is God's word, completely accurate and reliable.

I fully realize that there are plenty of people out there who do not believe the Bible. I am happy to debate the authority and reliability of the Bible. But not here. That would be a different book. If you don't believe the Bible, we need to have a totally different conversation. For the purpose of this book, I am starting with the assumption that you agree that the authority of the Bible is a settled question.

It's like: I used to be an officer in a Political Action Committee. When we produced advertisements or flyers for the general public, we would present arguments why they should vote for our candidates. We'd explain why we believed the policies we supported were good and why this was important. But when we got together for strategy meetings, we didn't discuss whether the policies we were promoting were good for the country. Everybody there already agreed on that. We didn't need to convince each other. What we needed to do was figure out which candidates agreed with us, and what the most effective way was to get them elected.

When Christians are talking to non-Christians, we debate which faith is true. But when we talk among ourselves, we consider that a settled question and go on to discuss the implications and details of our faith. This book is intended for people who already believe the Bible to be at least mostly true.

2.5.   Literal or figurative?

I'm a software engineer by profession, so I take a pretty hard-headed approach to anything I read.

I read the Bible the same way I read any other book. Many people read the Bible completely differently from the way they read "ordinary" books. They read the Bible expecting every sentence to be dripping with deep, inner meaning. They work on the assumption that everything is symbolic and spiritual.

For example, I once read an article based on Luke 22:36-38.

Jesus is speaking to his disciples, and he says, "He who has no sword, let him sell his garment and buy one." And the disciples reply, "Lord, look, here are two swords."

I understood those verses to mean that Jesus advised the disciples that they would need to be able to defend themselves, and they replied that they did indeed have a couple of weapons. But this writer explained that the two swords symbolized the authority of the church and the authority of the government. He went on a long discussion about the relationship of church and state, picking apart each word in these verses.

I certainly don't read computer books that way. When I read, say, "If the status light is yellow, this indicates a paper jam," I take this to mean that there is a yellow light on the printer, and that this means that paper is stuck in the printer. I don't start asking, "What does the color yellow mean to me?"

At worst, sometimes people take this "spiritual" approach because they can't or won't accept the plain, literal meaning. For example, they read a description of a miracle, like God sending the flood in Noah's day to destroy the world. They don't believe that this really happened, so they look for the "spiritual meaning" of the story. What is the writer trying to tell us about the nature of God and man? What do the flood waters represent? What does the ark represent? Etc.

Maybe they don't like what the Bible says. Like, they read a condemnation of some action as sin, but they see nothing wrong with that particular action. Maybe they do it themselves. They discard the plain, literal meaning and search for a "deeper", "spiritual" meaning that avoids acknowledging that this action is a sin.

Not only does this let them read whatever meaning they want into the text, but at the same time they can look down on those who take the plain meaning as being in a lower spiritual state because they cannot grasp the deeper meaning.

Sincere Christians often look for such spiritual meanings because they expect the Bible to be too deep for simple, mundane statements. They have been taught that the Bible has many layers of meaning, that there is always more to be learned from any verse, and so they search for these hidden inner meanings.

With all due respect, I politely say, No. I work on the assumption that the Bible means what it says and says what it means.

When I read, for example, that Jesus "came to a city of Samaria which is called Sychar" (John 5:4), I understand that to mean that Jesus got out of his chair, went out the door, and walked to a region called "Samaria" and to a city named "Sychar". I assume that these are real places that could be found on maps of the time, that people lived there, that they had roads and buildings, etc. I don't ask what "Sychar" symbolizes or what inner spiritual meaning this verse may be trying to communicate.

I suppose I should clarify two things here.

First, There may be some deep spiritual significance to the literal meaning. If you are familiar with the history of the Jews and Samaritans, you may know that the two groups hated each other. Jews rarely traveled through Samaria, but would instead take long detours to avoid it. It is perfectly fair and indeed quite interesting to ask, "Why did Jesus go to Samaria?"

However, this deeper meaning only exists if we first accept the literal meaning. If Jesus didn't really travel to Samaria, but this is just a story to express a spiritual truth, that spiritual truth would be considerably watered down if there was no reality behind it. It's all well and good to say, "You should renounce racism and reach out to people of all colors and backgrounds." But such a message is much more persuasive if you have actually done this yourself. To say, "You all should do this. Have I ever done it? Of course not, I wouldn't associate with those smelly, ugly people. But you should" -- well, that's not quite as effective, is it?

Second, I am not saying that the Bible does not use any figurative or symbolic language. Of course it does. When I say that I take the Bible literally, I don't mean that literally! Again, I read the Bible just like I read any other book. Some statements are clearly presented as being literal. Like, "Jesus went to Samaria". Other statements are clearly presented as figures of speech. Like, "Let the rivers clap their hands; Let the hills be joyful together before the Lord" (Psalms 98:8). I don't suppose that the rivers had hands and clapped. It's poetry. Jesus's parables are all clearly presented as being symbolic language. When he says, "The Kingdom of Heaven is like a mustard seed ..." (Matthew 13:31), he isn't saying that the Kingdom of Heaven *is* a mustard seed, but that, in a certain way that he goes on to explain, it is *like* a mustard seed. The mustard seed is a symbol.

Such symbolic language is not unique to the Bible. People often talk as if the Bible is the only book ever written that uses symbolic language, and so we must use a whole different set of thought processes to understand it than we use in "real life".

No. We all use symbolic language and figures of speech all the time. Sometimes the symbolic nature of our speech is obvious. When someone says, "It was raining cats and dogs today", of course I don't suppose that domestic animals were literally falling out of the sky, but that this is a colorful, symbolic way of saying that it was raining very hard. Sometimes the symbols are more subtle. When someone says, "We should try a different tack", this is a reference to sailing ships: "tacking" is sailing at a slight angle to the wind; it is a way of sailing as close to straight into the wind as you can. I suspect many people use that phrase without even realizing it is figurative speech or knowing the history.

I pulled a random book off my shelves to see how much figurative language I could find. I picked the history section of my library because history books have more narrative, but within that section I just grabbed the first one I could find. (You keep your books arranged by subject too, don't you?)

The book I picked was David McCullough's *John Adams*. In the very first paragraph I found this statement:

Packed ice in the road, ruts as hard as iron, made the going hazardous.

Do you think the ruts in the road were literally "hard as iron"? Probably not.

On the third page I found:

… he [John Adams] relished long walks and time alone on horseback. Such exercise, he believed, roused the animal spirits.

Did Adams really believe that walking brought dead animals back to life? Of course the writer meant the vigor within Adams himself.

A little later on the same page he says that Adams was "great-hearted", he was "not a man of the world", and "Patriotism burned in him like a blue flame." Did Adams literally have a blood-pumping organ bigger or stronger than that of most people? Did he come from another planet? Was there a blue fire inside his body?

And so on. Read any book and you are likely to find many statements which are not intended to be taken literally. Your friends make figurative statements in conversation every day.

Usually we have little problem distinguishing literal statement from figurative statements. It's obvious which is which. When we are reading or speaking to people we separate the literal from the figurative almost automatically, with barely a moment's thought.

To be fair, sometimes we get confused, particularly when reading material about an unfamiliar subject.

I work in the computer business. Computer books often use analogies to human thinking processes to explain how the computer works. We often casually say things like, "The computer expects the address to include a zip code." Does the computer really "expect" things to happen in the same way that a human being would expect something? No. What we mean is that the software does not work correctly if the data does not meet certain conditions. We'll say, "The computer remembers the last number typed in ..." Does the computer "remember" things in the same way that a human being remembers things? No. What we mean is that the value is stored electronically and is retrieved when it is needed. And so on.

Sometimes the way computer people use such figurative language leads people who are not knowledgeable about how computers work to incorrect impressions. Our casual talk about the computer "thinking" has led to thousands of science fiction stories that depict computers and robots as intelligent creatures who think and imagine. And of course, who plot to take over the world.

Computer professionals use figurative language, analogies, and metaphors with a clear picture in mind that this language is not literal, but rather a way of describing a complex or unfamiliar reality in comprehensible terms. Sometimes people who are not knowledgeable about computers can be confused, not sure what language is literal and what is figurative.

The same can be true of some sections of the Bible. When the Bible talks about things that are part of normal human experience, we have little difficulty distinguishing literal statements from figurative statements. When the Bible talks about things outside our normal experience, like when it talks about angels and demons and Heaven and Hell, it can be difficult. When we read cryptic descriptions of such things, are these literal descriptions of something outside our experience, or figurative language intended to tell us about their purpose rather than a literal physical description? It can be hard to say.

In 1970, Hal Lindsey wrote a book on prophecy, *The Late Great Planet Earth*, that presented a ground-breaking insight for interpreting some Bible prophecies, especially the book of Revelation. These prophecies include many descriptions of apparently bizarre monsters and strange places and objects. Most commentators before Lindsay interpreted these descriptions as highly symbolic. For example, consider the description of the locusts in Revelation 9:7-10, with phrases like "The shape of the locusts was like horses prepared for battle. On their heads were crowns of something like gold, and their faces were like the faces of men ..." Traditional commentators interpreted the horses, crowns, men's faces, and so on as symbols, and tried to figure out what each represented.

But what if, Lindsay said, God showed John things that would happen in our own time, 2000 years in John's future? Suppose God showed him, say, a war involving tanks and airplanes and bombs. How could John describe technologies far in advance of his own time? He might not understand much of what he saw. Even if he was smart enough to understand it or if God explained it to him or gave him miraculous understanding, he still wouldn't have the words in ancient Greek to describe it to others. Lindsay points out that John often uses the word "like". In the description of those locusts, for example, he uses the word "like" eight times. John does not say that the locusts *were* horses with men's faces, but that they were "like horses" and their faces were "like men's faces".

Revelation uses the phrase "something like" in many other places, too. For example, Revelation 8:8 says, "*something like* a great mountain burning with fire" and Revelation 15:2 says, "I saw *something like* a sea of glass". Etc.

I disagree with a lot of Lindsay's ideas, and I suspect he'd like to take back many things he said in the 1970s in light of subsequent historical events. This isn't a book about prophecy, however, so we need not get into that part of it. I think this basic insight of Lindsay's is valid and useful. At least some of Revelation is John describing things outside of his own experience: maybe future technology, maybe the supernatural.

2.6. Consistency

I work on the assumption that the Bible is internally consistent.

Again, I am reading the Bible just as I would read any other book. When I am reading instructions on how to use a computer, and on page 42 I read something that sounds different from what I read on page 27, my first response is not, "This book is full of contradictions!" No, my first thought is, "I must not be understanding this correctly." Long before I conclude that the manufacturer of a computer product got it wrong in their own book about how to use that product, I thoroughly explore the possibility that I'm reading it wrong.

Thus, I reject the approach that seeks to "resolve" apparent contradictions in the Bible by saying "this is the Old Testament view while that is the New Testament view" or "this is what Isaiah believed versus that is what Job believed". I work on the assumption that God knew what he was saying when he inspired the Bible, and that he didn't change his mind or realize later that he'd made a mistake.

If two statements in a book sound to me, on first reading, like they contradict each other, I look for some way to resolve the contradiction. First I re-read both statements carefully. Perhaps on my first reading I misread one (or both).

I look at the larger context. For example, two sentences might use the same word to refer to different things in a different context. To construct a silly example, suppose you read an article about the history of a newspaper publisher. In one place they say, "We buy new paper every day and never keep paper more than a week." In another place they say, "The paper has been at this location for over 50 years." Is that a contradiction? Is the paper kept for 50 years or for just one week? But of course in this example the resolution is obvious: In the first case "paper" refers to the material they print on, while in the second "paper" refers to the company.

Two statements may be referring to different times or places. If I read in one place that Russia is ruled by a tsar and in another that it is ruled by the communist party and in another that it is ruled by an elected president, there is no contradiction if I understand that this is talking about three different times in history.

This sort of caution is especially true when we are reading about something far away from our own experience. And Heaven and Hell are far away from any living human's experience. Perhaps what sounds like a contradiction would be quickly resolved if only we knew a little more.

2.7. Comprehension

To many atheists, if something in the Bible doesn't immediately make sense to them, they declare that the Bible is full of errors and contradictions. To many Christians, if something in the Bible doesn't immediately make sense to them, they declare that it is a profound spiritual mystery requiring special knowledge to decode, or that is beyond all human understanding.

Both responses are simplistic. We should consider the possibility that we might need to think about something for more than 10 seconds before coming to a conclusion.

If you were reading the instruction book for a new electronic gadget and came to a statement that was not clear, it is unlikely that your immediate response would be to conclude that this book was full of hopeless nonsense, or that the statement should not be taken literally but must be a profound comment on the mysteries of life. The rational person would read it again, check other parts of the book, try to follow the instructions as he understands them and see what happens, and so on.

2.8. Whims

Finally, what may seem like an obvious statement for anyone who takes the Bible seriously: We can't simply dismiss Bible verses that we don't like.

The Bible says lots of things that aren't very popular today. Too bad. When judgment day comes, it won't be the Supreme Court that I have to answer to. It won't even be the Academy Award committee.

The Bible says lots of things that make me uncomfortable. Too bad. The universe does not bend to suit my whims.

2.9. Scope

It turns out that a lot of what the Bible has to say about Eternity is wrapped up in prophecies about the future. Much of the discussion of Eternity is in Revelation and in prophecies in the Old Testament.

Eternity is a complicated enough subject without getting into prophecy, too. So in this book, I'll avoid discussing prophecy. Even when we are looking at verses that are part of a prophecy, I'll avoid talking about the prophecy and try to limit the discussion to Eternity.

2.10. Certainty

In this book I present some unconventional theories about Eternity.

Frankly, the Bible does not tell us a lot about Eternity. Reasonable people can read the Bible and come away with different conclusions. Perhaps God wants us to wonder and study. Perhaps we don't need to know.

There are some things I say here that I am quite sure of, and some that I suggest cautiously. There are many places where ... well, someone once said, "I was pleased that I was able to give him a complete and accurate answer. I said, 'I don't know'." (I think this comes from Mark Twain, but I was unable to track it down.)

There are many places in this book where I find it impossible to draw a firm conclusion. All is can say is, "Here are some popular theories", or "Here are some plausible interpretations of the text." I'm sure some readers would prefer me to just say, "This is how it is." But that wouldn't be honest. I'm not going to say I know when I don't.

I try to identify my level of certainty about various theories I propose. But I encourage you to study the Scriptures and think for yourself.

Here's how I think the game should be played: I quote verses and present logical arguments and say how I think they fit together and what conclusions we can draw. You read the verses for yourself and think for yourself and see if you agree. Maybe read what others have said and see whose arguments you find more convincing. I like to think I'm a smart and fair-minded guy, but I encourage you not to believe anything just because I say so.

2.11. Bible Versions

Except where otherwise specified, all Bible quotes used in this book are from the New King James Version.

Any translator of the Bible – or of any other book, for that matter – must struggle between a strictly literal rendering of the original text, and something that is readable and understandable in the target language. The New King James translators made the decision to generally err on the side of strict rendering. This makes it a good translation for serious study. Arguably this makes it not the best for more casual reading as the English is sometimes a bit awkward.

In some places I used the New International Version, because the English tends to read more smoothly and be easier to understand. I have labeled these quotes "(NIV)".

3. Plan of Attack

Okay, preliminaries done. Let's get to the point.

What got me started on this study was that I noticed that the Bible uses a number of different words and phrases for places in Eternity: Hades, Hell, the Lake of Fire and so on for "bad places"; Heaven, Paradise, New Jerusalem and so on for "good places". People generally assume that these are all many names for just two places: Heaven and Hell. I came to question if this was true, or if the Bible might be talking about more than just two places.

So here's the strategy I'll follow for the rest of this book.

First, I'll briefly talk about how one gets to the good place or ends up in the bad place. This is a necessary foundation for understanding the nature of these places.

Second, I'll list all the words and phrases that the Bible uses for places in Eternity. We'll investigate what it says about each, and discuss which are different names for the same place and which are names for different places.

Third, we'll discuss details about some of these places that would have distracted from the "tour", and general issues not directly related to specific places or place names. (Some writers come up with a useful approach to a subject and then get addicted to it, insisting on staying with it after it has outlived its usefulness. I don't want to fall into that trap.)

Finally, I'll wrap up with a summary of my understanding of how this all hangs together.

Let's go.

4. Saints & Sinners

4.1. Getting In

If you asked most people how one gets to Heaven, they'd say, "by living a good life".

Some believe that as long as you don't do something really bad, like murder or child abuse, you'll go to Heaven.

Others think that your good deeds must outweigh your bad deeds. One could question how this is counted. Does helping an old lady across the street outweigh using a curse word? How many children do you have to rescue from burning buildings to outweigh one case of child abuse? If you murder someone, but then you save another person's life, does that cancel out? But one might suppose that God knows exactly how many points, plus or minus, each action is worth.

People seem to think that this idea comes from the Bible. Which is funny because the Bible quite plainly says that this is *not* how one gets into Heaven.

> Ephesians 2:8-9 For by grace you have been saved through faith, and that not of yourselves; it is the gift of God, not of works, lest anyone should boast.

Salvation is not gained by doing good works: it is gained by faith. Faith in what, exactly?

John 3:16 For God so loved the world that He gave His only begotten Son, that whoever believes in Him should not perish but have everlasting life.

We must have faith in God's only son, Jesus Christ.
What about him? Does it just mean believing that he lived? No. The problem is this:

Romans 3:23 All have sinned and fall short of the glory of God.

Romans 6:23 For the wages of sin is death, but the gift of God is eternal life in Christ Jesus our Lord.

God doesn't grade on a point system. God's standard is perfection. Any sin, no matter how small it seems to us, is sufficient to condemn us to Hell. And of course we have all sinned. Any honest person would have to admit that he has committed *some* sin: Maybe you haven't killed anyone, but almost everyone has stolen something at some point in his life, looked at pornography, lied his way out of trouble, etc.
But there is a way out.

Romans 10:9-10 ... if you confess with your mouth the Lord Jesus and believe in your heart that God has raised Him from the dead, you will be saved. For with the heart one believes unto righteousness, and with the mouth confession is made unto salvation.

Romans 10:13 For whoever calls on the name of the Lord shall be saved.

All we need to do to escape the penalty for our sins is to believe that Jesus died on the cross as payment for our sins, and to accept Christ's offer of salvation.
God says that our sins mean that we deserve to die. But then he takes the penalty for our sins himself.
Salvation is a free gift. All we have to do is accept it.
If you have not accepted Christ's offer of salvation, don't worry about the rest of this book right now! Get your life right with God first. You can worry about everything else later.

4.2. Good Works, Reprise

People often get confused about faith versus works. Perhaps this is because the Bible does indeed talk about doing good works.

James 2:18 Show me your faith without your works, and I will show you my faith by my works.

Once a person is saved, he should do good works. But that is not how you get saved. That is the result of being saved.

Someone once said that the formula is not "faith + works = salvation", but "faith = salvation + works".

It's like ... at my last job the company had a book of rules that employees were required to follow. Things like, "No drinking alcohol during work hours", "You must complete a timesheet every week saying how many hours you have worked on each project", and "You must call in to the office if you are too sick to come to work."

Suppose you wanted to get a job with this company. How would you go about getting this job? Suppose you started following all the company rules: You don't drink during working hours, you fill out a timesheet every week, and you call into the office whenever you're sick. Would you then receive the benefits of having a job with this company? Would they start sending you paychecks and contributing to your 401k? Not likely. If you kept mailing in those timesheets and calling in sick they might eventually call the police and charge you with harassment.

No, the way you get a job is by applying for a job, having them formally offer you a position, and you accepting it. Following the rules is something you are expected to do *after* you get the job.

Of course many of the rules are good to follow of themselves. Like, it's a good idea not to get drunk during work hours no matter where you work. But you don't get the job because you followed all the company rules.

Salvation works the same way. You are saved by accepting God's offer of salvation. Once you are saved, *then* God expects you to follow all the rules. Many of the rules are good things to do whether you are saved or not. But you are not saved by following the rules.

(The analogy does break down at one point: If you don't follow the company rules, eventually you will be fired. But you do not lose your salvation because you failed to follow God's rules. He always forgives.)

4.3. Believing, Reprise

There is a difference between believing in Christ, in the sense of believing that he lived, and believing in Christ in the sense of accepting his offer of salvation.

> James 2:19 You believe that there is one God. Good! Even the demons believe that—and shudder. (NIV)

Satan and his demons believe that God and Christ exist. I presume they believe it more certainly than any human on Earth today, because they have personally seen them. But they are not saved because they have not accepted Christ's offer of salvation.

Christians sometimes talk about this as a difference between "head knowledge" and "heart knowledge".

Let me put it this way. Years ago, back when the idea of "computer networks", i.e. getting computers to communicate with each other, was new, I worked for a company that sold computer systems. We needed a good networking system to package with our products and sell to our customers. We bought several and tried them and none of them worked well. Then we bought a system from what at the time was a new company that few people had heard of, and it worked great! I said to myself, I should buy stock in this company. As others learn about their product, these people are going to make a fortune!

You can probably guess what comes next. I didn't buy stock in the company, and they did indeed go on to make billions of dollars.

I had plenty of knowledge about the company. I knew exactly how to go about cashing in on their success. But I never acted on that knowledge. In the end, my knowledge did me no good at all – except to give me this amusing little story. Knowing that the stock existed and was likely to increase in value was an essential first step. But I had to buy the stock to actually benefit from it.

In the same way, believing that Jesus Christ lived is an essential step. But it's not sufficient. You must accept his offer of salvation to actually benefit from it.

4.4. Terminology

The Bible has many different words to describe those who will live in eternity with Christ, versus those who will not. In this book, I will refer to these two groups as the "saved" and the "unsaved". I avoid using words like "righteous" and "sinners" to avoid confusion between the idea of being saved and the idea of doing good works.

5. Itinerary

5.1. Complexity

The Bible has many names for places in Eternity. I have come to the conclusion that Eternity has a more complex geography than is generally assumed. There are not just two places, Heaven and Hell. There are many.

You may be tempted to say, "Why would God have created more than two places? A good place for the good people and a bad place for the bad people. What more is needed?"

I reply: Because we are talking about real life and not about a children's story. If you or I decided to invent a religion that we thought made good sense and would be nice to believe and easy to win converts for, no doubt we could come up with something simple and easy. But that's not how real life is. Real life is often messy and complicated.

Maybe this happens on other subjects, but it seems that often when a Christian is trying to explain what the Bible says to non-Christians, they demand a simple answer. If the Christian is unable to give the Biblical position in one easy-to-understand sentence, the person complains that he refuses to give a straight answer, or that the

Bible is incoherent. Any complexity is labeled a "contradiction" and taken as an argument that the whole thing is a fraud.

Even when one Christian is talking to another, we say that we expect to find great depth in Scripture, but at the same time we expect all questions to have an easy answer, or we practically give up in despair.

Like, in some places the Bible says that we have free will; in other places it says that God has predestined those who will be saved. The non-Christian says, "I don't see how both things could be true. The Bible contradicts itself and so is a bunch of meaningless hogwash." But many Christians are not much better. Some will say, "I don't see how both things could be true. So I'll pick the one I like best and ignore the other." Others will say, "It's an unknowable mystery. Perhaps God will explain it all to us when we get to Heaven."

As I've said, I develop computer software for a living. One day I was chatting with a group of other software developers and the conversation rolled around to a story that was in the news at the time about bugs found with the software used in some voting machines: apparently they were miscounting the votes. One of the people in the conversation said that he couldn't imagine how you could have bugs in such a simple program. After all, he said, what does it take? You just get a list of all the votes and count how many for each candidate. He could write such a program in an hour, he insisted. At the time I asked if he was a student or had actually worked on real-life projects. (He never did answer.) In a school problem, sure, the students might well be told that the homework for today is to create a screen that has two buttons, one labeled "Republican" and one labeled "Democrat", and they should count the number of times that each button is pressed and display the totals. I could write that program in an hour, too. But in real life, the problem is far more complicated. There are normally many offices on the ballot, not just one. Different voters may get different lists of candidates to vote for: while all the voters may be voting for president, only those within the city limits may vote for mayor; voters in district 1 will have one set of candidates for Congress while voters in district 2 will have another set. Etc. In some races you can only vote for one candidate, but in other races you may be able to vote for many candidates. For example, if there are five members on the school board, you may be allowed to vote for up to five candidates from the list. Some voters may choose to vote in some races but not in others. You probably need to provide some way for the voter to fix a mistake or change his mind before his vote is "committed". You have to provide for write-in candidates who are not listed on the ballot. Etc, etc.

My point is that if you can just make up a problem – like an exercise for a class in school – sure, you can make it clean and simple. You can make everything completely consistent, with no special cases or exceptions or missing details to be filled in later.

But real life is often complex.

In this book I talk about the "geography of Eternity". I think that many people leap to the conclusion that two places that the Bible describes must be the same place because of similarities in the descriptions. For example, the Bible talks about unsaved people being sent to the Lake of Fire. It also talks about unsaved people in Hades and describes that as a place of fire. Many Christians therefore conclude that Hades and the Lake of Fire are the same place. That's not an absurd idea, there are clearly similarities in the descriptions, but a few similarities are not proof that they are two names for the same place.

Consider the geography of Earthly places. Someone might describe Norway as a place of snow and ice populated primarily by light-skinned people. One could give a similar description of Canada. Would it be fair to conclude that therefore Norway and Canada must be two names for the same place?

There are times when a place has two names, of course. A place will often have different names in different languages. That's a very relevant point here, where we are looking at one book written in Greek -- the New Testament -- and another in Hebrew -- the Old Testament.

Sometimes one name describes a big place, and another name describes a smaller section of that place. Or sometimes a name can mean both the big place *and* a section of that place, depending on context. "America" is often used as another name for "the United States". People from, say, Argentina, sometimes object that they are "Americans" despite the fact that they are not part of the United States.

At the beginning of this section I said that one might be tempted to object, "Why would God have created two places that both are X?" In one sense I could counter, "Why would people have created two places that are both snowy and have light-skinned people, like Norway and Canada?" Put that way the question sounds rather silly. There are all sorts of geographical and historical reasons why Norway and Canada are two different countries. If you don't know the reasons, it is certainly fair to ask what they are. It would not be fair to say that because you don't know any such reasons, that therefore this must be two names for the same country and that anyone who claims they are two different countries is just trying to confuse you and make things complicated.

As we go through the list of places in Eternity, we'll be discussing which might be two names or descriptions for the same place and which are different places, what each place is like and what purpose it serves.

5.2. A list of places

Here is a list of places in Eternity that the Bible names. We'll be going through these place names in detail in the next chapter. But this chart gives you an overview.

A few words of explanation about the chart:

"Testament" indicates whether this word or name is found in the Old Testament or the New Testament.

"Hebrew/Greek Word" is the word found in the original text of the Bible. Old Testament words are Hebrew; New Testament words are Greek. (With one exception that we'll get to.)

"Origin" gives some notes about where the word comes from. We'll discuss these further in the body of the text.

"Translated" is the words or words used to translate the Hebrew or Greek in most English translations.

Places in Eternity

Testament	Hebrew/Greek Word	Origin	Translated
OT	Sheol	"unseen", "hidden"	grave, hell
OT	Abaddon		destruction
OT	bur		pit
NT	Gehenna	Valley of Hinnom	hell
NT	Abyss		bottomless pit, deep, depths
NT			lake of fire
NT	Hades	Greek mythology	Hades, hell
NT	Tartarus	Greek mythology	hell
n/a		Latin "edge"	Limbo
n/a		same root as "purge"	Purgatory
OT	Shamayim		heavens
NT	Ouranos		heaven
NT	kolpon tou Abraam		Abraham's bosom
NT	kaines ierousalem		New Jerusalem
NT	basileia toon ouranon		Kingdom of Heaven
NT	basileia tou theou		Kingdom of God
NT	paradeisos	"garden", "park"	Paradise
NT	ouranos kainos kai ge kaine		New heaven and new Earth

A few notes:

The word "Abaddon" is a Hebrew word and is primarily found in the Old Testament. It occurs once in the New Testament, in Revelation 9:11. It is the only word on this list that is found in both the Old and New Testaments. This is not particularly surprising, as the Old Testament is written in Hebrew and Aramaic while the New Testament is in Greek. We wouldn't normally expect to find Hebrew words in a Greek text or vice versa.

The words "Limbo" and "Purgatory" are not found in the Bible. They are words invented by later writers to describe ideas derived from their understanding of the Bible.

The word "Hell" is an old Anglo-Saxon word used by pagans for their idea of the underworld. It is not derived from any Hebrew or Greek word or any word appearing in the Bible. It was adopted by Christians about the 8th century AD. As noted in the chart, it is used in many English translations to translate several Hebrew and Greek words: Sheol, Gehenna, Hades, and Tartarus.

5.3.   Translations

And right away we have a problem.

Let me make clear that I have great respect for the people who made our English translations. The King James in its day, the New King James today, the Revised Standard, New American Standard, the original New International, and no doubt others that I'm less familiar with are masterpieces of translation. To an amazing extent, they faithfully reproduce the meaning of the original text while being clear and highly readable in English.

That said, I will pick a quibble with how they translated some of these words.

A number of these words are proper names for places.

When someone translates a document that includes a place name, they usually come up with a rendering in English that tries to reproduce the sound of the name in the original language. This is called a "transliteration".

If the place has a well-known name in the target language, a translator may use that name rather than the name from the original language.

Names often have roots and histories. That is, a name often has a meaning. Perhaps you know the origins or your own name or the name of your town. Occasionally, if the meaning behind the name is important, or if people regularly think of the meaning of the name, translators may really translate the name, that is, use English words that reflect the meaning of the words in the original language rather than the sound.

For example, suppose you were translating a book from Arabic and came across the place name "al-Quds". You might translate this as I just did there – al-Quds – as a reasonably good English approximation of the sound of the name in Arabic. Or you might translate the meaning of the name, and write "The Holy City". Or you might use the name of the city that is most familiar to English-speaking people, and translate it "Jerusalem". (That is, al-Quds is what Arabs call the city that Jews and most Westerners call Jerusalem.)

What translators normally *don't* do is sometimes transliterate the name, sometimes translate it, and sometimes use a more-familiar place name. That would be confusing. Readers could easily be left unsure whether this was one place or several places, or whether this was a specific place or a description of a kind of place.

Yet for some reason, that is precisely what translators have done with many of the names for places in Eternity.

For example, the Old Testament includes a number of references to a place called, in Hebrew, "Sheol". In English Bibles, sometimes they transliterate this as "Sheol", sometimes they translate it "the grave", and sometimes they use the word "Hell". The same translation will often use multiple words to translate the same place name. In some cases they will use two different words to translate it in the same verse or paragraph.

At least four different Hebrew and Greek words are translated to the single English word Hell: Sheol, Gehenna, Hades, and Tartarus. Given that the Bible uses four different place names, we should be cautious about assuming that these are all the same place. Indeed, as I've said, I conclude there are at least two and probably three places here. But it can be difficult for someone reading an English translation to even consider the possibility that there is more than one place under discussion when the translator uses the same English name for what in Hebrew and Greek are four different names.

I don't know why the translators did this. I find it very

confusing. Perhaps if I talked to them they'd have some very good reason.

To get around this problem, in this book I routinely refer back to the Greek and Hebrew words. When I quote verses, I put a transliteration of the original Greek or Hebrew word in square brackets after whatever word the translators used. For example, I'll write "the grave [Sheol]", meaning that if you look in your English Bible, it will say "the grave", but this is a translation of the Hebrew word "Sheol".

6. A Tour of Eternity

All that said, let's start going through the places.

6.1. Sheol

The word "Sheol" occurs 64 times in the Bible. It comes from a root meaning "hidden" or "unseen".

In English Bibles, it is sometimes translated as "Sheol", and sometimes as "the grave" or "Hell".

The Hebrew word "qeber" is also translated "grave". But the two have very distinct meanings. Nowhere does the Bible talk about souls in qeber. Nowhere does the Bible talk about a body being buried in Sheol. Sheol is always used in the singular, as the proper name of a place. Qeber is used generically, sometimes in the singular and sometimes in the plural. So a qeber is a physical hole in the ground or a tomb where you place a body. Sheol is a place where the soul goes after death.

Let's look at what the Bible tells us about Sheol.

Psalms 9:17 The wicked shall be turned into hell [Sheol], And all the nations that forget God.

Job 24:19 As drought and heat consume the snow waters, so the grave

[Sheol] consumes those who have sinned.

The unsaved go to Sheol when they die.

Some believe that the saved – at least those who lived before Christ – also went to Sheol:

Psalm 89:48 What man can live and not see death? Can he deliver his life from the power of the grave [Sheol]?

This can be taken to mean that everyone goes to Sheol, not just the unsaved.

Perhaps you recall the Bible story of Joseph being so hated by his brothers that they sold him into slavery and told their father Jacob that he had been killed by a wild animal. Toward the end of this story we are told:

Genesis 37:34-35 Then Jacob tore his clothes, put sackcloth on his waist, and mourned for his son many days. And all his sons and all his daughters arose to comfort him; but he refused to be comforted, and he said, "For I shall go down into the grave [Sheol] to my son in mourning." Thus his father wept for him.

Jacob was saved -- if you have any doubt, Jesus says so, Matthew 8:11 -- but he expected to go to Sheol.

Hezekiah was one of the few good kings of Judah, faithful and obedient to God. He was surely saved.

Isaiah 38:9-10 This is the writing of Hezekiah king of Judah, when he had been sick and had recovered from his sickness: I said, "In the prime of my life I shall go to the gates of Sheol; I am deprived of the remainder of my years."

Nevertheless, Hezekiah expected to go to Sheol.

On the other hand, it is possible that these statements are not meant literally. Psalm 89 may not mean that all men go to Sheol, but rather than no man can save himself from Sheol by his own power – he must trust in God.

Likewise, when Jacob and Hezekiah talk about going to Sheol, note that they are both in the midst of extreme situations: Jacob thought his son was dead, and Hezekiah was facing an early death himself. Perhaps both men talked of "going to Sheol", not literally, but rather as a way to say how terrible their situation was. Much like people today say that they "went through Hell".

> Psalm 49:15 But God will redeem my soul from the power of the grave [Sheol], For He shall receive me.

> Psalm 86:12-13 I will praise You, O Lord my God, with all my heart, And I will glorify Your name forevermore. For great is Your mercy toward me, And You have delivered my soul from the depths of Sheol.

God will "redeem" or "deliver" the souls of the saved from Sheol. This could mean that God does not allow the souls of the saved to go to Sheol in the first place, but the plainer reading is that they go there and then he gets them out.

> Job 14:13-14 "Oh, that You would hide me in the grave [Sheol], That You would conceal me until Your wrath is past, That You would appoint me a set time, and remember me! If a man dies, shall he live again? All the days of my hard service I will wait, Till my change comes.

Job expected to go to Sheol when he died, but then at some future date be "changed" and leave Sheol. While this is not very explicit, it sounds like a resurrection or a transition to some other state in eternity.

On the other hand, there are some verses that seem to say that the saved do *not* go to Sheol.

> Proverbs 15:24 The way of life winds upward for the wise, That he may turn away from hell [Sheol] below.

> Proverbs 23:13-14 Do not withhold correction from a child, for if you beat him with a rod, he will not die. You shall beat him with a rod, and deliver his soul from hell [Sheol].

(Side note: Some people point to this verse and say it condones child abuse. The point of this verse is that, by disciplining your children, you may save them from Hell. The part about beating them with a stick doesn't mean that this should be the normal mode of punishment. The whole point of the proverb is that, *even if* the only way to get through to your child is to beat him with a stick, this would be better than doing nothing and letting him go to Hell. The intent could be that this is the last resort, or it could be rhetorical exaggeration.)

A common theory among Christian scholars is that before Christ died on the cross to pay the penalty for our sins, no one could go to Heaven, because the price of admission had not yet been paid. So instead Sheol was divided into two parts, an unpleasant place for the unsaved and a pleasant place for the saved. Then after Christ's death he went to Sheol and led these people into Heaven.

Nowhere does the Bible say this outright, but there are some verses that are consistent with this theory. The closest to saying this, and probably where the idea comes from, is:

> Ephesians 4:8-9 Therefore He says: "When He ascended on high, He led captivity captive, And gave gifts to men." (Now this, "He ascended"— what does it mean but that He also first descended into the lower parts of the earth?

That is, some Christians interpret this to mean that after Christ's death, he went to Sheol, released the souls of the Old Testament saved, and took them to Heaven.

Some also point to:

> 1 Peter 3:18-20 For Christ also suffered once for sins, the just for the unjust, that He might bring us to God, being put to death in the flesh but made alive by the Spirit, by whom also He went and preached to the spirits in prison, who formerly were disobedient, when once the Divine longsuffering waited in the days of Noah, while the ark was being prepared, in which a few, that is, eight souls, were saved through water.

They say that this means that after his death Christ preached to the souls imprisoned in Sheol, and then freed them.

Personally I find the Scriptural evidence for this theory weak, but I don't have a better theory.

The Ephesians passage doesn't say that the captives he freed were in "the lower parts of the earth", nor is it clear that the "lower parts of the earth" here means Hell or Sheol. These verses could just as well mean that Christ freed humanity in general from the penalty for their sins, and that Christ left his glory in Heaven to come to Earth to do this.

The Peter passage is even weaker. It specifically says that the spirits he preached to "formerly were disobedient". That sounds like it means the unsaved, not the saved. Apparently Christ preached to the souls of the unsaved dead. Exactly why he did this and what sort of message he preached is not spelled out, but it's not evidence for this theory.

He might have preached a message of triumph, declaring to those who hated God that they had lost and God had won. But if they are in Hell, don't they already know that?

Perhaps he gave them one last chance to repent, or gave those who had never heard of God an opportunity to be saved. This conflicts with the doctrine that there is no "second chance" after death, but one could debate that. (See section 8.8.) If Ephesians 4 is talking about the same event, that would indicate that some unsaved dead were given a final chance at this time.

He may have given them an opportunity to repent, knowing that they would not take it. People in rebellion against God continue in rebellion. Thus he could demonstrate his justice and mercy. The catch to this is that it seems implausible that he could preach to many millions of unsaved dead, and not one would repent.

Even the most righteous person is disobedient at times, so one could argue that the intent here is to say that these are saved people who were in Sheol because they could not merit Paradise on their own righteousness, and had to wait for Christ to come save them. But "the disobedient" are contrasted with Noah's family. The most natural reading is that these were the unsaved, perhaps specifically the unsaved who lived before the Flood.

Curiously – to me anyway – most of the references to Sheol make one of two points.

The first point is that Sheol has an appetite that is never satisfied.

Proverbs 27:20a Hell [Sheol] and Destruction [Abaddon] are never full.

Proverbs 30:16 The grave [Sheol], The barren womb, The earth that is not satisfied with water — And the fire never says, "Enough!"

Isaiah 5:14a Therefore Sheol has enlarged itself and opened its mouth beyond measure;

This is certainly literally true: Everyone dies. Death is never satisfied, but always wants more.

It is not clear to me if there is some deeper meaning here or if this is intended as a plain statement of fact.

The second point is that God can see Sheol.

> Proverbs 15:11 Hell [Sheol] and Destruction [Abaddon] are before the Lord; So how much more the hearts of the sons of men.

> Psalm 139:8 If I ascend into heaven, You are there; If I make my bed in hell [Sheol], behold, You are there.

> Amos 9:2 "Though they dig into hell [Sheol], from there My hand shall take them; Though they climb up to heaven, from there I will bring them down;

In context, the point in all these verses is that there is no way to escape from God; there is nowhere you can go that he does not see and where he cannot reach you. Even a place as remote as Sheol is still within God's field of vision.

Traditionally, people have thought of Hell as being beneath the surface of the Earth. If by Hell we mean Sheol, there is Scriptural justification for this.

> Job 11:7-8 Can you search out the deep things of God? Can you find out the limits of the Almighty? They are higher than heaven— what can you do? Deeper than Sheol— what can you know?

> Amos 9:2 Though they dig into hell [Sheol], From there My hand shall take them; Though they climb up to heaven, From there I will bring them down;

> Isaiah 14:13-15 For you have said in your heart: 'I will ascend into heaven, I will exalt my throne above the stars of God; I will also sit on the mount of the congregation On the farthest sides of the north; I will ascend above the heights of the clouds, I will be like the Most High.' Yet you shall be brought down to Sheol, To the lowest depths of the Pit.

Sheol is consistently referred to as being "deep" and "downward" and a place that one "digs down to".

I suspect this is figurative. Describing Heaven as "up" and Sheol as "down" may simply be a metaphor. It may be literal. Sheol may literally be somewhere beneath the surface of the Earth.

The idea of Hell or Sheol being underground seems a little … naïve. But then again, why so? We certainly can't say that we know there is no such place underground. It's 4,000 miles from the surface to the center of the Earth. The deepest holes in the world are not quite 8 miles deep: the Kola Superdeep Borehole in Russia and the Al Shaheen oil well in Qatar. That's 1/5 of 1%. We've barely scratched the surface. Of course there are other ways to learn what's down there besides digging a hole, like studying shock waves that have passed through the Earth. But we know very little about the interior of the Earth, and we don't really know what Sheol would look like if we saw it.

6.2. The Pit

The word "pit" is a translation of the Hebrew word "bur". This word occurs 70 times in the Bible. Most of these uses are referring to a literal pit, that is, to a hole in the ground. But a few places are clearly referring to something else.

In a prophecy about the city of Tyre, Ezekial says:

> Ezekial 26:20 [T]hen I will bring you down with those who descend into the Pit, to the people of old, and I will make you dwell in the lowest part of the earth, in places desolate from antiquity, with those who go down to the Pit, so that you may never be inhabited; and I shall establish glory in the land of the living.

In a prophecy about Egypt, he says:

> Ezekial 31:15-16 Thus says the Lord God: 'In the day when it went down to hell [Sheol], I caused mourning. I covered the deep because of it. I restrained its rivers, and the great waters were held back. I caused Lebanon to mourn for it, and all the trees of the field wilted because of it. I made the nations shake at the sound of its fall, when I cast it down to hell [Sheol] together with those who descend into the Pit; and all the trees of Eden, the choice and best of Lebanon, all that drink water, were comforted in the depths of the earth.

Ezekial 32:17-32 lists many nations now destroyed as all in "the Pit".

The Pit is associated with Sheol, but it does not appear to be the same place. Ezekial talks about those "cast down to Sheol *together with* those who descend into the Pit". This would be very odd phrasing if these were two names for the same place.

Job 33:23-24 If there is a messenger for him, A mediator, one among a thousand, To show man His uprightness, Then He is gracious to him, and says, 'Deliver him from going down to the Pit; I have found a ransom';

Psalm 30:3 O Lord, You brought my soul up from the grave [Sheol]; You have kept me alive, that I should not go down to the Pit.

Psalm 49:8-9,15 For the redemption of their souls is costly, And it shall cease forever — That he should continue to live eternally, And not see the Pit. ... But God will redeem my soul from the power of the grave [Sheol], For He shall receive me."

Again, the Pit is associated with Sheol.

While there is some ambiguity whether the saved go to Sheol, there is no indication that the saved do not go to the Pit.

These verses may be consistent with the theory that there is a "good part" and a "bad part" to Sheol. The "Pit" may be a name for the "bad part". But then Ezekial's talk of those going to Sheol along with those going to the Pit would not make sense. We wouldn't say "those going to Europe and also those going to France", we'd say something more like "of the people going to Europe, some are going to France".

So the Pit is not just another name for Sheol. But ... that's as far as we seem to be able to get. The verses quoted above are all that the Bible tells us about the Pit.

It is possible that the "Pit" of the Old Testament is related to the "Bottomless Pit" of the New Testament. But let's be careful: Even though both use the word "pit", that's an English word. It's the translation of two different words, one Hebrew, "bur", and one Greek, "abyss". The meanings are similar enough that it is possible that "abyss" is the Greek translation of "bur". But it's hard to say.

6.3. Hades

Hades is a Greek word found in the New Testament. It is used eleven times. Most English Bibles transliterate it as "Hades", though some translate it "Hell".

The word Hades comes from Greek mythology. To the ancient Greeks, Hades was the place of the dead. It was divided into two parts. The evil went to a place of torment called Tartarus. The good went to a paradise called the Elysian Fields or Elysium.

This concept of Hades as having a "good place" and a "bad place" parallels the common Christian theory of Sheol we discussed in section 6.1. Does this mean anything or prove anything?

The ideas that the soul survives death, and that the good should be rewarded and the evil punished, are not particularly far out or unusual ideas. Greek religion was strictly works-based. There is no concept of salvation by grace; it is entirely a matter of what you deserve based on what you did in life. The similarity of the Greek idea of eternal reward for the good and eternal punishment for the evil to the teachings of the Bible may simply reflect the common human concept of justice. People of almost all cultures and religions believe that good should be rewarded and evil punished. If you believe in an afterlife, it is no great stretch of the imagination to suppose that injustices on Earth will be corrected in Eternity.

These ideas come from God in at least the general sense that God created all human beings with an intuition for justice. God may simply have chosen a Greek word that would bring to the minds of listeners and readers the idea that he wants to relate.

Or, maybe God moves to give many cultures some idea of divine truths, to give everyone a chance. God may have revealed something to the Greeks. Perhaps this was all part of God's plan for them. Maybe God sent prophets to the Greeks who are not remembered today because the Greeks ignored them. Or maybe God revealed the truth to them in some other, less direct, way. In either case, they only listened to a few scattered ideas. As neither the Bible nor Greek history tell us just where Greek ideas about Hades came from, all we can do is speculate.

Alternatively, it's possible that the Christian idea of Sheol being divided into a good place and a bad place is borrowed from Greek mythology, and then Bible verses cherry-picked to support it. As I think we saw in section 6.1, the Bible verses to back up this theory are not particularly clear or explicit. Still, the idea seems to be there. I mention this possibility just to acknowledge it -- I doubt it's true.

That is, maybe the similarity in these details was essentially a coincidence, and God took advantage of the coincidence. Or maybe God worked directly to plant these ideas in Greek thought. Some Christians believe that there are no coincidences, that everything is part of God's plan. Others believe that God does not direct everything but works through circumstances.

The book of Acts relates a sermon by Peter. He quotes from a psalm of David, Psalm 16:10.

> Acts 2:27-31 "For You will not leave my soul in Hades, Nor will You allow Your Holy One to see corruption." ... Men and brethren, let me speak freely to you of the patriarch David ... being a prophet, and knowing that God had sworn with an oath to him that of the fruit of his body, according to the flesh, He would raise up the Christ to sit on his throne, he, foreseeing this, spoke concerning the resurrection of the Christ, that His soul was not left in Hades, nor did His flesh see corruption.

This passage tells us a couple of interesting things.

First, the Old Testament verse uses the Hebrew word "Sheol". When Peter quotes this verse he says it in Greek, using the Greek word "Hades". Peter did not invent this translation: Many Jews at that time used a Greek translation of the Hebrew Old Testament called the Septuagint. (The word "Septuagint" means "seventy", because according to tradition the translation was made by 70 scholars in 70 days. It is often abbreviated LXX, the Roman numerals for 70.) The Septuagint always translates "Sheol" as "Hades". The fact that Peter used this translation indicates that he endorsed it, and the fact that it appears in our inspired Bible implies that God endorses it.

So it seems very likely that when the New Testament talks about Hades this is referring to the same place that the Old Testament calls Sheol. Hades is apparently the Greek translation of the Hebrew word Sheol. In this case we have reason to believe that these are two names for the same place.

There is some debate about the origin of the word "Hades". According to the Greek philosopher Plato, the common belief was that it came from a word meaning "unseen". Plato then went on to argue that this was wrong, and it really meant "knowledge". But the fact that Plato found it necessary to explain away this theory indicates that it was the generally accepted one. If the common belief that Plato dismisses is in fact correct, then the Greek word Hades may have a similar root meaning to the Hebrew word Sheol – recall that Sheol comes from a Hebrew root word meaning "unseen". Of itself that doesn't prove anything, but it's interesting.

Second, the plain reading is that Jesus was in Sheol/Hades. If God did not "leave" him in Hades, that implies that he was in Hades. But unlike an ordinary person, Jesus had the power to leave Hades.

> Matthew 11:20-24 Then He [Jesus] began to rebuke the cities in which most of His mighty works had been done, because they did not repent: "… And you, Capernaum, who are exalted to heaven, will be brought down to Hades; for if the mighty works which were done in you had been done in Sodom, it would have remained until this day. But I say to you that it shall be more tolerable for the land of Sodom in the day of judgment than for you."

The unsaved go to Hades. That's consistent with Hades being another name for Sheol.

Revelation describes several series of judgments or disasters. One of these series is the "seven seals". The first four of the seven seals are represented by men on horses, often called the "Four Horseman of the Apocalypse". The last of these is:

> Revelation 6:7-8 When He opened the fourth seal, I heard the voice of the fourth living creature saying, "Come and see." So I looked, and behold, a pale horse. And the name of him who sat on it was Death, and Hades followed with him. And power was given to them over a fourth of the earth, to kill with sword, with hunger, with death, and by the beasts of the earth.

So the fourth horseman is Death, and Hades follows him. (If Hades is also on a horse, then there are really "Five Horsemen of the Apocalypse" rather than "Four". But whatever.)

This could simply mean that the disasters – the wars, famines, and wild animals – result in people dying, and these people then go to Hades. That is, they die and their deaths are followed by Hades. There may be something more specific meant in the context of prophecy. But we are not given any further information.

> Rev 20:11-15 Then I saw a great white throne and Him who sat on it, from whose face the earth and the heaven fled away. And there was found no place for them. And I saw the dead, small and great, standing before God, and books were opened. And another book was opened, which is the Book of Life. And the dead were judged according to their

works, by the things which were written in the books. The sea gave up the dead who were in it, and Death and Hades delivered up the dead who were in them. And they were judged, each one according to his works. Then Death and Hades were cast into the lake of fire. This is the second death. And anyone not found written in the Book of Life was cast into the lake of fire.

This happens after the Millennium. Again, I don't want to get into prophecy, but most commentators see the Millennium as a future event. As the word "millennium" means a period of 1000 years, then if this period hasn't started yet, we are talking about events at least 1000 years from now.

So at some time in the future, there will be a great judgment. At that time all the dead in Hades will be judged, and the unsaved will be thrown into the Lake of Fire. (See section 6.8.)

Then Death and Hades will themselves be destroyed in the Lake of Fire.

Thus, Hades is a temporary place. Hades will not exist forever. After the Millennium, it will be destroyed, and the unsaved will be "transferred" to the Lake of Fire.

This indicates that Hades and the Lake of Fire are two different places. Hades cannot be thrown into itself. Furthermore, Hades will be destroyed, but as we shall see, the Lake of Fire exists forever.

You may ask, Why would God send people to Hades temporarily, and then later move them to the Lake of Fire? Why not just send them directly to the Lake of Fire? I wonder that, too. Unfortunately, the Bible does not spell it out. If we knew more, perhaps this would make perfect sense. It might be like asking, "Why do we send children to elementary school before they can go to college?" Or perhaps more relevantly, "Why are criminals kept in the county jail before they are sent to the penitentiary?" Each has its own purpose and its own structure.

How are Hades and the Lake of Fire different and what is the function of each?

As Hades is temporary and the Lake of Fire is permanent, perhaps God is using Hades as a temporary "holding place" until he creates the Lake of Fire. As we shall see, some day God is going to destroy the Earth (see section 6.13). If Hades/Sheol is literally inside the Earth (section 6.1), then Hades cannot continue to exist after the

Earth is destroyed – either God would have to destroy it first or the process of destroying the Earth would also destroy Hades. So Hades would have to be temporary.

The Bible describes the destruction of the Earth and the destruction of Hades in separate places in the text. Maybe the destruction of Hades is a by-product of the destruction of the Earth, and this just isn't spelled out. Or maybe Hades is not inside the Earth, and the destruction of the Earth has nothing to do with the destruction of Hades. I think that if the two events were tied together, the Bible would say this. But not necessarily.

Of course all this raises the question why God didn't just create the Lake of Fire to begin with. Was he not able to for some reason? Presumably not for lack of power – I don't suppose God couldn't find the necessary materials or got tired trying to build it! But maybe there is something about the nature of the Lake of Fire that it would not be appropriate for God to create it or use it before a certain point in history.

If Hades indeed has two parts, then once the saved are taken out of the "good part" – whether that is past or future -- Hades is at least half obsolete. So maybe it serves its purpose for a time, and then is replaced with the permanent place.

Another possibility is that the unsaved are kept in Hades until the final, Great White Throne judgment of Revelation, and then they are sent to the Lake of Fire. That is, Hades is where the unsaved are kept before judgment, and the Lake of Fire is where they go after judgment. It's like the difference between the jail where an accused person is kept while awaiting trial, and the prison he is sent to after he is convicted. The pre-trial jail is not a place of punishment, but a place to hold him while his guilt and any punishment are decided. The jail is near the court house so the accused can be brought to the court to participate in his trial, while the prison is often in a remote location to make escape more difficult. Etc. I'm not saying those particular differences are paralleled in Hades and the Lake of Fire, but just using them as an analogy. If Hades is pre-judgment and the Lake of Fire is post-judgment, then there may be differences between the two that reflect this difference in purpose.

We are told that demons are condemned to the Lake of Fire, but there is no clear discussion of demons being sent to Hades.

Demons are imprisoned in the Abyss (see section 6.5) and Tartarus (see section 6.7). Maybe these places are parts of Hades, but if not, it could be that Hades is just for people. Both people and demons ultimately end up in the Lake of Fire.

One final footnote on this section: These verses seem to be describing "the sea", "death", and "Hades" as three physical places. It seems unlikely that someone who dies at sea has a different status in the afterlife than someone who dies on land. It's possible that "the sea" here does not refer to literal lakes and oceans but to some place in Eternity, perhaps a place that is somehow related to the oceans or is like the oceans. But I know of no other Bible verses that describe such a place. Likewise, Death – the Greek word "thanatos" – is used here as if it was a place. There are a few other Bible verses that speak of Death in a way that it could be understood to be a place rather than an event or state. But frankly, I just don't see enough information to go anywhere with this.

> 1 Corinthians 15:55-57 "O Death, where is your sting? O Hades, where is your victory?" The sting of death is sin, and the strength of sin is the law. But thanks be to God, who gives us the victory through our Lord Jesus Christ.

Jesus saves us from Hades. This gets us back to the question of whether the saved go to Hades. This could mean that Jesus saves people from ever being sent to Hades, but the more natural reading is that people are sent to Hades, but then Jesus gets them out. Note that Jesus rescuing people from Hades parallels his rescuing them from death. He doesn't prevent the saved from dying. The saved die, but Jesus turns it into something positive. So the paragraph makes the most sense if we take it to mean that the saved go to Hades, and then Jesus turns this into something positive.

Revelation quotes Jesus as saying:

> Revelation 1:18 I am He who lives, and was dead, and behold, I am alive forevermore. Amen. And I have the keys of Hades and of Death.

This might simply mean that Jesus has power over Hades and death. But why would Jesus use the word "key"? That implies the ability to lock something up or to open it after it's locked.

If Jesus freed the saved from Hades, he had to be able to "unlock the cells". Saying that Jesus has the keys to Hades is consistent with the idea of Jesus freeing the saved from Hades at his resurrection.

Another quote from Jesus:

> Matt 16:18 ... on this rock I will build My church, and the gates of Hades shall not prevail against it.

The gates of Hades will not stand against Christ's church.

Christians often read this verse as a promise of Christ's protection: when the forces of Hell attack, Christ will protect us from them so that they "shall not prevail" against us.

But this makes little sense when we consider the presence of the word "gate". A gate does not attack. A gate is something to keep intruders or attackers out. It is a defense.

This could fit the theory that Jesus released the saved from Hades. The gates of Hades were locked, but they could not stand against him.

Except that this verse says that the gates of Hades will not stand against the Church, not that they will not stand against Christ. And if Christ released the Old Testament saved from Hades, he must have done this himself, not through the Church.

So I think the more likely understanding of this verse is that he is using "Hades" here somewhat figuratively to mean those who are doomed to be sent to Hades, that is, Satan and his followers. He is saying that the Church should be on the attack, and that we will attack Satan's fortress and batter down his gates, and the gates of Hell shall not stand against us.

There is one more passage that talks about Hades: Luke 16:19-31. We'll discuss this in section 6.12, Abraham's Bosom.

6.4. Gehenna

Gehenna is the English translation of the Greek translation of a Hebrew word.

The Hebrew is "Ge Hinnom". "Ge" means "valley" and "Hinnom" was a man's name, so the name means "Hinnom's Valley".

In some places it's called "Ge Ben Hinnom", or "Hinnom's Son's Valley".

When Greek-speaking people arrived, they translated it to Greek as "Ge-enna". From this we get the English word "Gehenna".

This valley was outside Jerusalem. It had an interesting history:

2 Chronicles 28:1-3 Ahaz ... did not do what was right in the sight of the Lord, as his father David had done. For he walked in the ways of the kings of Israel, and made molded images for the Baals. He burned incense in the Valley of the Son of Hinnom, and burned his children in the fire, according to the abominations of the nations whom the Lord had cast out before the children of Israel.

2 Chronicles 33:5-6 [King Manasseh] built altars for all the host of heaven in the two courts of the house of the Lord. Also he caused his sons to pass through the fire in the Valley of the Son of Hinnom; he practiced soothsaying, used witchcraft and sorcery, and consulted mediums and spiritists. He did much evil in the sight of the Lord, to provoke Him to anger.

When the Bible says "he caused his sons to pass through the fire", it means that he had his sons burned alive as human sacrifices to pagan gods. The Valley of Hinnom was a place where people sacrificed their children to Molech.

When the Jews turned away from idol worship, the history of what had been done there led the people to have a very low opinion of the place. So they took to using it as a garbage dump. Not only ordinary garbage, but also the bodies of dead animals and sometimes bodies of executed criminals were dumped there.

Some sources say that fires were kept burning there constantly to consume the garbage, though this is disputed.

Just as English has become the international language of commerce and science today, so in the period between the Old and New Testaments, Greek became the international language. Jewish writers in this period came to use the word Gehenna as a word for a place of eternal punishment for the unsaved. The "earthly" Gehenna was a place of fire and decaying bodies where the most horrible sins were committed. Seeing it and thinking of its history might well have brought to mind images of Hell.

Most English Bibles translate Gehenna as "Hell".

The Greek word Gehenna is used twelve times in the Bible.

Eleven of those times are quotes from Jesus; the last is by James.

> Mark 9:47-48 And if your eye causes you to sin, pluck it out. It is better for you to enter the kingdom of God with one eye, rather than having two eyes, to be cast into hell [Gehenna] fire — where "Their worm does not die, And the fire is not quenched."

This is a quote from Jesus. He makes a number of statements very similar to this: it is better to give up something in this life that leads you into sin then to end up in Gehenna.

> Matthew 5:22 But I say to you that whoever is angry with his brother without a cause shall be in danger of the judgment. And whoever says to his brother, 'Raca!' shall be in danger of the council. But whoever says, 'You fool!' shall be in danger of hell [Gehenna] fire.

Jesus point, here and elsewhere, was that even the sins that we think of as trivial and unimportant are enough to send someone to Hell. "Raca" was considered a very bad swear word. I'm sure you can think of comparable words in English. There were even laws against saying this word. But, Jesus says, even using a mild insult like "fool" unjustly is a sin.

Together these verses tell us that Gehenna is a place of fires that never go out and worms that never die, and a life of sin will end in Gehenna.

> Luke 12:4-5 And I say to you, My friends, do not be afraid of those who kill the body, and after that have no more that they can do. But I will show you whom you should fear: Fear Him who, after He has killed, has power to cast into hell [Gehenna]; yes, I say to you, fear Him!

Going to Gehenna is something to be feared far more than dying. If you are killed and you are saved, you will spend eternity in paradise, but if you die and you are not saved, you will spend eternity in Gehenna.

> Matthew 23:15 Woe to you, scribes and Pharisees, hypocrites! For you travel land and sea to win one proselyte, and when he is won, you make him twice as much a son of hell [Gehenna] as yourselves.

> Matthew 23:33 Serpents, brood of vipers! How can you escape the condemnation of hell [Gehenna]?

> James 3:6 And the tongue is a fire, a world of iniquity. The tongue is so
> set among our members that it defiles the whole body, and sets on fire
> the course of nature; and it is set on fire by hell [Gehenna].

The James verse doesn't add much to our knowledge of Gehenna, but I include it because it's the only mention of Gehenna by someone other than Jesus.

The word Gehenna has something of an odd history. It's the name of an earthly place that people adopted as a name for an eternal place. If the story ended there, I'd be inclined to say that we should avoid using the word as it creates a potential for confusion. But Jesus used the word, so apparently he considered it a legitimate term.

There is some ambiguity if the saved go to Sheol. But there is no mention of the saved ever going to Gehenna. It is purely a place for the unsaved.

6.5.   Abyss

The word "Abyss" is a Greek word that is normally translated "pit", "bottomless pit", or "the deep".

It is used nine times in the Bible. Several of those occurrences are close together, so that adds up to just five general places where it's mentioned.

> Rom 10:6-7 "Do not say in your heart, 'Who will ascend into heaven?'"
> (that is, to bring Christ down from above) or, "'Who will descend into
> the abyss?'" (that is, to bring Christ up from the dead).

The question is clearly rhetorical: the answer is "no one". Christ had the power to come to Earth and to raise himself from the dead, but that no human could have done these things. This could just mean that: no one has the power to bring Christ down from Heaven or up from the Abyss. Or it could mean that no one has the power to go to Heaven or the Abyss period, and thus could not hope to bring Christ down or up.

Either way, the Abyss is presented as some sort of opposite of Heaven.

> Luke 8:27-28,31 And when He [Jesus] stepped out on the land, there met
> Him a certain man from the city who had demons for a long time. And
> he wore no clothes, nor did he live in a house but in the tombs. When

he saw Jesus, he cried out, fell down before Him, and with a loud voice said, "What have I to do with You, Jesus, Son of the Most High God? I beg You, do not torment me!" ... And they begged Him that He would not command them to go out into the abyss.

The Abyss is a place where God might send a demon. It seems that the Abyss is a prison for demons.

Revelation 20:1-3 Then I saw an angel coming down from heaven, having the key to the bottomless pit [Abyss] and a great chain in his hand. He laid hold of the dragon, that serpent of old, who is the Devil and Satan, and bound him for a thousand years; and he cast him into the bottomless pit [Abyss], and shut him up, and set a seal on him, so that he should deceive the nations no more till the thousand years were finished. But after these things he must be released for a little while.

Satan will be imprisoned in the Abyss. This is consistent with demons being imprisoned in the Abyss.

Revelation 11:7 When they finish their testimony, the beast that ascends out of the bottomless pit [Abyss] will make war against them, overcome them, and kill them.

The context is that God sends "the Two Witnesses" to preach to men. "The Beast" comes from the Abyss and kills them. Many commentators believe that this "beast" is the same person who elsewhere is called the "Antichrist".

So this Beast comes from the Abyss. This could mean that the Abyss is the home or headquarters of the Beast. But if the Abyss is a prison for demons, how could it also be the headquarters of someone who is in league with Satan? That seems inconsistent. Either demons are imprisoned there, or they rule there. They wouldn't do both.

A possibility is that when it says that the beast "ascends out of the Abyss" this means that the Beast was a prisoner in the Abyss and was released. Or escaped, I suppose. My first thought is that an omnipotent God could prevent anyone from escaping his prison. But then, nothing says that God personally guards the prison. People fail all the time, even when they are doing God's work. It seems plausible that angels are fallible also. If angels guard the Abyss, perhaps a demon imprisoned there could outsmart them and escape.

Finally, it is possible that the Beast did not literally come from the Abyss, but that this is a figurative way of saying that he is in league with the demons imprisoned there. We sometimes say that something is "heavenly" without meaning that it literally came from Heaven. But this seems unlikely from the phrasing in this case.

(Note: These next verses use both the Greek word "abyss", which appears to be a name for a specific place, as well as the general word for "pit", "phreatos". The New King James translates "abyss" as "bottomless pit" and "phreatos" as simply "pit".)

> Revelation 9:1-5 Then the fifth angel sounded: And I saw a star fallen from heaven to the earth. To him was given the key to the bottomless pit [Abyss]. And he opened the bottomless pit [Abyss], and smoke arose out of the pit [phreatos] like the smoke of a great furnace. So the sun and the air were darkened because of the smoke of the pit [phreatos]. Then out of the smoke locusts came upon the earth. And to them was given power, as the scorpions of the earth have power. They were commanded not to harm the grass of the earth, or any green thing, or any tree, but only those men who do not have the seal of God on their foreheads.

Some terrifying creatures come from the Abyss and attack the enemies of God.

If these are demons released from prison, why would they attack the enemies of God rather than his friends? It is possible that God manipulates them to do his will. The Bible describes many occasions when God used evil people to accomplish his purposes. A number of times in the Old Testament he used evil kings to punish Israel when they sinned. He used Judas as part of his plan for Jesus to be killed and then come back from the dead. Etc. It may be that God releases some number of demons from prison and then, when they think they are doing something to attack God, he outsmarts them and maneuvers them into doing exactly what he wants.

I think it is more likely, though, that while the Abyss includes a prison, it is more than just a prison. It is something bigger than that. A police station houses prisoners, but it is also a base of operations for the police. Fort Knox is an army base, but is also used to safeguard the United States gold reserve. I suspect the Abyss is like a police station or a fort: it is some kind of headquarters, where an army of God is based, and this also contributes to it being a secure place to hold prisoners.

Is the Abyss the same as Sheol? I don't think so. There's really no reason to think they are the same place. Nowhere does the Bible say that they are the same. There's the obvious fact that they have two different names, and those names have no obvious relationship – the two words do not have similar meanings or similar origins. The Abyss is described as a prison for demons and possibly a sort of "army base" for God's soldiers. Sheol is described as a place where the souls of dead people go. There's no mention of demons in Sheol or of the souls of humans in the Abyss.

I do see one argument that they are the same place. Recall that Romans 10:7, quoted at the beginning of this section, asks who could "descend into the Abyss ... to bring Christ up from the dead". This implies that when Christ died on the cross he went to the Abyss. This could mean that the Abyss is where people go when they die. Furthermore, if Christ went to Sheol when he died, and he went to the Abyss when he died, that might mean that these are two names for the same place. Obvious rebuttals are that he might have visited two places, and that his visit to the Abyss had nothing to do with where ordinary people go when they die. (By "ordinary people", I mean people who are not God.)

Is it possible that they are the same place? Yes. But there's little reason to think so.

6.6. Abaddon

Abaddon is a Hebrew word meaning "destruction". It occurs seven times in the Bible. One of these (Job 31:12) uses the word as a conventional noun. The other six use it as the name of a place in Eternity. Let's go through each of these.

Several mention Abaddon with Sheol.

Job 26:6 Sheol is naked before Him, And Destruction [Abaddon] has no covering.

Proverbs 15:11 Hell [Sheol] and Destruction [Abaddon] are before the Lord; So how much more the hearts of the sons of men.

Job 28:20-22 From where then does wisdom come? And where is the place of understanding? It is hidden from the eyes of all living, And concealed from the birds of the air. Destruction [Abaddon] and Death say, "We have heard a report about it with our ears."

Psalm 88:9b,11 Lord, I have called daily upon You; ... I have stretched out my hands to You. Shall Your lovingkindness be declared in the grave [Sheol]? Or Your faithfulness in the place of destruction [Abaddon]?

The point of these verses is to tell us that God sees everything, and that his love extends everywhere. Abaddon (and Sheol) are understood to be remote, far from normal human understanding.

Proverbs 27:20 Hell [Sheol] and Destruction [Abaddon] are never full; So the eyes of man are never satisfied.

We discussed this verse in section 6.1 on Sheol.

Frankly, none of this tells us very much about Abaddon. Most Jewish and Christian writers conclude from these verses that Abaddon is a place, somehow related to Sheol. The Babylonian Talmud, an ancient Jewish book, says that Abaddon is another name for Sheol.

But: In 6.5 we discussed the Abyss. Recall that an army of creatures that resemble locusts come out of the Abyss to attack the enemies of God. Then we are told:

Revelation 9:11 And they had as king over them the angel of the bottomless pit [Abyss], whose name in Hebrew is Abaddon, but in Greek he has the name Apollyon.

Just as "Abaddon" is a Hebrew word meaning "destruction" or "destroyer", so "Apollyon" is the Greek word for "destroyer". So for the benefit of readers who speak Greek but not Hebrew, John gives the Greek translation of Abaddon. If Revelation had been written in English, he would have said "in English he has the name Destroyer".

So in Revelation Abaddon is not a place, but an angel, a creature.

Some commentators say Abaddon is the Antichrist, or Satan himself. But if he is either, why is he doing God's will? It sounds more like Abaddon is an angel whom God has placed in charge of the Abyss. The fact that he is called an "angel" and not a "demon" indicates that he is serving God, not Satan.

Jehovah's Witnesses go in the opposite direction and say that Abaddon is another name for Jesus. But there's no solid Biblical basis for saying that. Just because he is leading an army that does God's will? Throughout the Bible God puts human leaders in charge of armies doing his will, and sends angels on missions for him. It's not like Jesus is the only possible being who can lead in God's name. Note the Bible says Abaddon is an "angel", not Christ.

So is Abaddon a place or an angel?

It's possible that this is simply a coincidence of names, that there is an angel with the same name as a place. Like "Indiana" is both the name of a U.S. state, and the first name of an adventurous archaeologist in a series of movies. When I say "coincidence" here, that could be literally true, that the two have nothing to do with each other. Or one may be named after the other, or they may be related in some way.

It could be that people are misreading the Old Testament when they understand Abaddon to be a place. Maybe they are jumping to conclusions just because Abaddon is mentioned in conjunction with a place, Sheol. If the Abyss is another name for Sheol or is a place related to Sheol, perhaps the references to "Sheol and Abaddon" are intended to be references to a place and its ruler or a person associated with it, like saying "Britain and the Queen". I find that theory tempting, but pre-Christian Jewish sources all appear to understand Abaddon to be a place, not a person, and it's a stretch to suppose that they all misread the Hebrew scriptures.

In any case, the Abaddon of Revelation is one of just three angels who are named in the Bible, along with Michael and Gabriel. Four if you include Satan. (There is also mention of "Baalzebub", but this appears to be another name for Satan.) (I'm speaking of the Protestant Bible here. Catholic Bibles include several additional books that name additional angels.)

6.7. Tartarus

Tartarus is another word borrowed from Greek mythology. As we mentioned in the discussion of Hades, section 6.3, in Greek mythology Hades was divided into two parts, the Elysian Fields for the good and Tartarus for the evil.

The word is only used once in the Bible:

2 Peter 2:4 For if God did not spare the angels who sinned, but cast them down to hell [Tartarus] and delivered them into chains of darkness, to be reserved for judgment;

God imprisoned fallen angels in Tartarus.

Note that Tartarus is not described as a place of punishment per se, but rather as a place of imprisonment where these angels are held until the time of judgment.

The fact that God chose to use the Greek word Tartarus, which in Greek mythology is part of Hades, may mean that this Tartarus that he speaks of here is part of the real Hades. But not necessarily: he may have just considered the word Tartarus suitably descriptive of this place.

Tartarus is described as a prison for fallen angels and the Abyss is described as a prison for fallen angels, so they may be two names for the same place. Or God may have more than one prison. And why not? The United States has more than one prison. There are a variety of reasons for having more than one prison: In human terms, we have separate prisons for dangerous violent criminals than for people who have committed non-violent crimes. We have separate prisons for men than for women. Etc. If God has more than one prison, it may or may not be for similar reasons.

The main reason to suppose they are the same place is because they are both prisons for fallen angles. The main reason to suppose they are different places is because they have different names.

With just this one brief reference to Tartarus, it's difficult to conclude much about it.

6.8. Lake of Fire

The phrase "Lake of Fire" is used four times, all of them in Revelation.

> Revelation 19:19-21 And I saw the beast, the kings of the earth, and their armies, gathered together to make war against Him who sat on the horse and against His army. Then the beast was captured, and with him the false prophet who worked signs in his presence, by which he deceived those who received the mark of the beast and those who worshiped his image. These two were cast alive into the lake of fire burning with brimstone. And the rest were killed with the sword which proceeded from the mouth of Him who sat on the horse. And all the birds were filled with their flesh.

In Revelation, the Beast and the False Prophet are the leaders of the enemies of God. "Him who sat on the horse" is Jesus. So Jesus defeats the forces of the Beast and the False Prophet and they are thrown into the Lake of Fire.

But curiously, the rest of the forces of evil are *not* thrown into the Lake of Fire at this time, but, we are told, are simply killed. It would seem, then, that they go to Hades until judgment day, a thousand years later after the Millennium, and at that time, when Hades is destroyed, then they are sent to the Lake of Fire. (See section 6.3.)

Why are the Beast and False Prophet sent to the Lake of Fire before everyone else? We'll get back to this question in a moment, but we need to go through some other verses first.

> Rev 20:7-10 Now when the thousand years have expired, Satan will be released from his prison and will go out to deceive the nations which are in the four corners of the earth, Gog and Magog, to gather them together to battle, whose number is as the sand of the sea. They went up on the breadth of the earth and surrounded the camp of the saints and the beloved city. And fire came down from God out of heaven and devoured them. The devil, who deceived them, was cast into the lake of fire and brimstone where the beast and the false prophet are. And they will be tormented day and night forever and ever.

Recall from section 6.5 that the Devil is imprisoned in the Abyss for 1000 years. When that time is over, he is released and leads a rebellion against God. God destroys this army. The Devil is cast into the Lake of Fire with the Beast and the False Prophet.

> Revelation 20:15 And anyone not found written in the Book of Life was cast into the lake of fire.

All the unsaved are thrown in the Lake of Fire.

> Revelation 21:8 But the cowardly, unbelieving, abominable, murderers, sexually immoral, sorcerers, idolaters, and all liars shall have their part in the lake which burns with fire and brimstone, which is the second death.

Again, the unsaved are thrown in the Lake of Fire.

As we mentioned in section 6.3, the Lake of Fire cannot be Hades. Hades is destroyed in the Lake of Fire. Hades is temporary, but the Lake of Fire is forever – we are told that the torment in the Lake of Fire lasts "forever and ever".

The Lake of Fire may be the same place as Gehenna (section 6.4). Both are places of fire that burns forever, where sinners are sent to be punished. I've said repeatedly in this book that when two places have different names, that is evidence of itself that they are two different places. We shouldn't assume that there can only be some small number of places in Eternity. But that thinking doesn't entirely apply here. "Gehenna" is a name; "Lake of Fire" is a description. "Gehenna" is used by Jesus when speaking to Jews, and it is a word that was familiar to Jews. "Lake of Fire" is used by John in Revelation when speaking to a wider audience, many of whom would not be familiar with the word Gehenna. There's a good reason why Jesus might have used a proper name while John used a description.

There is one other verse that doesn't use exactly the same phrase, but that I think is referring to the same place.

Matthew 25: 41 Then He will also say to those on the left hand, 'Depart from Me, you cursed, into the everlasting fire prepared for the devil and his angels.'

Jesus says that the unsaved will be sent to a place of everlasting fire. That fits what we're told about Gehenna and the Lake of Fire.

There's one new piece of information here: this place was "prepared for the devil and his angels". Revelation tells us that the Devil will be sent to the Lake of Fire; this tells us that fallen angels will be sent there also. This makes sense, we might have guessed it, but then there are lot of things that sound plausible and that we might have guessed that aren't true.

Many commentators make much of this point. They will say, "Hell was created for the devil and his demons – it was never intended for human beings." I don't think the last part of that is true. If Hell wasn't intended for human beings, than why is God sending human beings there? But at least part of the purpose of the Lake of Fire was to be the place where the devil and his demons were sent.

I said I'd get back to the question of why the Beast and the False Prophet are sent to the Lake of Fire before judgment day. It's possible that they are "special" because they are the leaders. But here's my theory. Most commentators believe that the Beast and the False Prophet are ordinary humans – very evil humans, like Hitler or

Blackmun, maybe worse, but humans nonetheless. But what if the Beast and the False Prophet are demons? There is no mention in the Bible of demons being sent to Hades. They are imprisoned in the Abyss and Tartarus, but there is no mention of them being sent to Hades. But we are told that they are sent to a place of everlasting fire. If the Beast and the False Prophet are demons, then it makes sense that they would not spend time in Hades, but would go straight to the Lake of Fire.

6.9. Kingdom of God

The phrase "Kingdom of God" is used 69 times, all in the New Testament.

Many people think that the "Kingdom of God" is something that will come when Jesus returns. Others think that it is another name for Heaven. They read verses like these:

> Mark 14:25 "Assuredly, I say to you, I will no longer drink of the fruit of the vine until that day when I drink it new in the kingdom of God."

At the Last Supper, Jesus tells his disciples that he will not drink wine again until some future day in the Kingdom of God. As he was killed the next day, that must mean Heaven or some future reign of Christ on Earth.

> Luke 13:28-29 "There will be weeping and gnashing of teeth, when you see Abraham and Isaac and Jacob and all the prophets in the kingdom of God, and yourselves thrust out. They will come from the east and the west, from the north and the south, and sit down in the kingdom of God."

At the time Jesus said this, Abraham, Isaac, and Jacob were all long dead. So it sounds like Jesus must be talking about Heaven (or some other place in Eternity).

So is the Kingdom of God another name for Heaven or a Millennial kingdom? No, it's not.

> Matthew 12:28 But if I cast out demons by the Spirit of God, surely the kingdom of God has come upon you.

Jesus said that the Kingdom of God "has come": it's here, on

Earth, now.

> Mark 9:1 And He said to them, "Assuredly, I say to you that there are some standing here who will not taste death till they see the kingdom of God present with power."

You don't have to die to see the Kingdom of God. It is not some place in Eternity or in the future. Everyone who was present with Jesus at that time is now dead, so they saw the Kingdom of God, 2000 years ago.

Christians often ask when the Kingdom of God will finally come to the Earth. The Pharisees asked Jesus that very question 2000 years ago:

> Luke 17:20-21 Once, on being asked by the Pharisees when the kingdom of God would come, Jesus replied, "The coming of the kingdom of God is not something that can be observed, nor will people say, 'Here it is,' or 'There it is,' because the kingdom of God is in your midst." (NIV)

The New King James says, "The kingdom of God is within you."

If you're waiting for the Kingdom of God – you missed it. It's already here. You cannot see it. It is not a place. It is inside human beings.

> John 18:36 Jesus answered, "My kingdom is not of this world. If My kingdom were of this world, My servants would fight, so that I should not be delivered to the Jews; but now My kingdom is not from here."

He doesn't say "Kingdom of God" here, just "my kingdom", but it appears to be the same idea. Again, the Kingdom of God is not a place. It is the community of believers.

How can we reconcile the verses that seem to say that the Kingdom of God is another name for Heaven with those that say it's here on Earth? It's not very hard. Like many apparent contradictions, the answer is: it's both.

The Kingdom of God is the Church. Not "the church" in the sense of a building, but the community of all believers. Jesus created it. The Old Testament saved are also part of it.

And it will continue into Eternity. Join now, and you don't just get a lifetime membership, you get an eternal membership. The Kingdom of God began on Earth 2000 years ago, but it will continue to exist in Eternity, because believers will live forever, starting here and continuing into Eternity.

6.10. Kingdom of Heaven

A similar phrase is "Kingdom of Heaven". These two phrases appear to be used interchangeably.

For example:

Matthew 8:11-12 And I say to you that many will come from east and west, and sit down with Abraham, Isaac, and Jacob in the kingdom of heaven. But the sons of the kingdom will be cast out into outer darkness. There will be weeping and gnashing of teeth

Luke 13:28 There will be weeping and gnashing of teeth, when you see Abraham and Isaac and Jacob and all the prophets in the kingdom of God, and yourselves thrust out.

The two verses say essentially the same thing, right down to specifically naming "Abraham, Isaac, and Jacob" and using the phrase "there will be weeping and gnashing of teeth". But note that Matthew says "kingdom of heaven" while Luke says "kingdom of God".

Matthew 18:3 Assuredly, I say to you, unless you are converted and become as little children, you will by no means enter the kingdom of heaven.

Luke 18:16 But Jesus called them to Him and said, "Let the little children come to Me, and do not forbid them; for of such is the kingdom of God."

Again, Jesus makes very similar statements, one about the Kingdom of Heaven, the other about the Kingdom of God.

Matthew 13:31-32 Another parable He put forth to them, saying: "The kingdom of heaven is like a mustard seed, which a man took and sowed in his field, which indeed is the least of all the seeds; but when it is grown it is greater than the herbs and becomes a tree, so that the birds of the air come and nest in its branches."

Luke 13:18-19 Then He said, "What is the kingdom of God like? And to what shall I compare it? It is like a mustard seed, which a man took and put in his garden; and it grew and became a large tree, and the birds of the air nested in its branches."

I find this the most conclusive. These appear to be excerpts from two different sermons or conversations. On both occasions, Jesus tells the same story about a mustard seed. But in one case he says it is like the Kingdom of Heaven, while in the other case he says it is like the Kingdom of God. It's one thing to give a similar description of two different places; it's another to tell the same story.

One last thing about the Kingdom of Heaven. Not really relevant but it's one of my favorite verses:

> Matthew 11:12 From the days of John the Baptist until now, the kingdom of heaven has been forcefully advancing, and forceful men lay hold of it. (NIV)

The Kingdom of Heaven is not for cowards or weak-willed people. It is for "forceful men".

So "Kingdom of God" and "Kingdom of Heaven" are two names for the same thing. But it is not a place: it is a group of people. While it will continue to exist in Eternity, it also exists here on Earth. And that's the last we'll say about it in this book. Having concluded that it is not a place, we find it is not relevant to the subject at hand.

6.11. Heaven

The word "Heaven" is used in both the Old and New Testaments. But it's two different words in the original that are both translated to the same English word. The Old Testament word is the Hebrew "shamayim". The New Testament word is the Greek "ouranos". For our purposes here we can discuss them together.

The word "heaven" is used in the Bible with at least three different meanings. (Note: In many of the following verses, we're not so much concerned with the point of the verse, but simply with side references to heaven.)

> Deuteronomy 11:11 but the land which you cross over to possess is a land of hills and valleys, which drinks water from the rain of heaven

> Acts 14:17 Nevertheless He did not leave Himself without witness, in that He did good, gave us rain from heaven and fruitful seasons, filling

our hearts with food and gladness

Psalm 104:12 By them the birds of the heavens have their home; They sing among the branches.

Job 35:5 Look to the heavens and see; And behold the clouds— They are higher than you.

Meaning number one: Heaven is the place that the rain comes from, and where we see birds and clouds. That is, heaven is the sky.

Genesis 22:17a blessing I will bless you, and multiplying I will multiply your descendants as the stars of the heaven

Deuteronomy 4:19 And take heed, lest you lift your eyes to heaven, and when you see the sun, the moon, and the stars, all the host of heaven, you feel driven to worship them and serve them, which the Lord your God has given to all the peoples under the whole heaven as a heritage.

Meaning number two: Heaven is the place where the Sun, Moon, and stars are. That is, heaven is outer space.

Deuteronomy 26:15a Look down from Your holy habitation, from heaven, and bless Your people Israel and the land which You have given us.

1 Kings 8:30 And may You hear the supplication of Your servant and of Your people Israel, when they pray toward this place. Hear in heaven Your dwelling place; and when You hear, forgive.

Psalm 103:19 The Lord has established His throne in heaven, And His kingdom rules over all.

Matt 5:34-35 But I say to you, do not swear at all: neither by heaven, for it is God's throne; nor by the earth, for it is His footstool; nor by Jerusalem, for it is the city of the great King.

Meaning number three: Heaven is where God lives and has his throne.
There may be a fourth way that the word "heaven" is used in the Old Testament:

Deuteronomy 10:14 Indeed heaven and the highest heavens belong to the Lord your God, also the earth with all that is in it.

Nehemiah 9:6a You alone are the Lord; You have made heaven, The heaven of heavens, with all their host,

"Highest heaven" in Deuteronomy 10:14 is actually "heaven of heavens" in the original Hebrew, the same words as Nehemiah.

There are only a handful of occurrences of the phrase "heaven of heavens" in the Bible, and none of them clearly identify just what it refers to. Like the ones I quoted, they all just say "God created the heaven of heavens" or "the heaven of heavens cannot contain God".

Most commentators think that "heaven of heavens" means the heaven of God's throne, i.e. the same as meaning number three. I've never found a suggestion that it is something other than one of the three meanings we've just discussed: sky, space, or God's home.

There is another discussion about Heaven which doesn't tell us a lot, but which is interesting mostly because of just one word:

2 Corinthians 12:2-4 2 I know a man in Christ who fourteen years ago—whether in the body I do not know, or whether out of the body I do not know, God knows — such a one was caught up to the third heaven. And I know such a man — whether in the body or out of the body I do not know, God knows — how he was caught up into Paradise and heard inexpressible words, which it is not lawful for a man to utter.

Paul describes a man who had a vision of Heaven or was physically taken up to Heaven. Many commentators say that this person was Paul himself and that he is trying to be modest. Whether he was talking about himself or someone else, I, like many others, find the most interesting thing about this brief account the word "third". What did Paul mean by saying this person saw the "third heaven"?

There are (at least) four theories about how the heavens were numbered.

Theory 1: Paul is referring to the three heavens we discussed above. This man was not taken to the sky or to outer space, but to the heaven of God's throne.

Theory 2: There are layers of outer space.

There were a variety of theories in ancient times about the structure of the universe. Some believed that the Earth was the center of the universe, the "geocentric theory"; others that the Sun was the center, the "heliocentric theory". The geocentric theory was more popular until the Middle Ages.

Ancient people knew there was a difference between planets and stars. They could see that the stars all stayed in the same place relative to each other, but that planets move against the background of the stars. They knew of five planets: Mercury, Venus, Mars, Jupiter, and Saturn. These are the planets that can be seen with the naked eye. The other planets were not discovered until after the telescope was invented: Uranus in 1781 and Neptune in 1846. (Pluto was discovered in 1930, but is no longer classified as a planet.)

By the way, contrary to popular belief, most ancient people did not believe that the Earth was flat. They knew that it was a sphere. Circa 250 BC, Eratosthenes of Cyrene even calculated the size of the Earth by measuring the lengths of shadows at different latitudes at the same time of day. He calculated the circumference of the Earth as 250,000 stadia, which comes to about 28,400 miles. The actual value is 24,900 miles, so he was off by less than 15%.

According to the geocentric theory, the Earth is at the center of the universe. The stars are on a giant sphere surrounding the Earth. The Sun, the Moon, and the planets move in orbits around the Earth, inside the sphere of the stars.

They saw sever layers between the Earth and the stars:

1: Moon
2: Mercury
3: Venus
4: Sun
5: Mars
6: Jupiter
7: Saturn

In the Intertestamental period – that is, the time between the writing of the Old Testament and the New Testament – a number of Jewish writers adopted this theory. The idea of Seven Heavens appealed to them because the number seven has Biblical significance: God rested on the seventh day after creation and established the seven-day week. The number turns up in various other places in the Bible, like Joseph prophesized seven years of famine, there were seven lamps in the tabernacle, etc.

Theory 3: Muslims and some Jews believed there were multiple levels of rewards in Heaven, speaking of Heaven here as the place where the saved go after death. People who were just barely good enough to make it into Heaven go to level one, those who are a little better go to level two, etc., with the most holy going to level seven.

The Koran, the Muslim holy book, includes a story of Mohammed being taken to Heaven by the angel Gabriel. In each level he meets a notable person from the Bible:

1: Adam
2: John the Baptist and Jesus
3: Joseph (the Old Testament Joseph)
4: Enoch
5: Aaron
6: Moses
7: Abraham

(Note that Jesus only made it to level two.)

Some Jews had similar theories. The Talmud describes seven Heavens. They linked each of the seven levels to a word used in the Bible in conjunction with the word "heaven" (except the first one). Namely:

1: Vilon (וילון), "curtain", not found in the Bible
2: Raki'a (רקיע), "firmament" or "expanse", Genesis 1:17
3: Shehaqim (שחקים), "clouds" or "skies", Psalm 78:23
4: Zebul (זבול), "residence", Isaiah 63:15
5: Ma'on (מעון), "habitation", Deuteronomy 26:15, Psalm 42:9
6: Machon (מכון), "site", "settled place", 1 Kings 8:39
7: Araboth (ערבות), literally "plains", "gorges", Numbers 22:1; figuratively "clouds" or "heavens", Psalm 68:4; "desert garden", Isaiah 51:3

Theory 4: There will be a series of three Earths and three Heavens over time.

This theory relates to the "Gap Theory". According to the Gap Theory, there is a large gap in time between Genesis 1:1 and Genesis 1:2.

Genesis 1:1 In the beginning God created the heavens and the earth.

Genesis 1:2 The earth was without form, and void; and darkness was on the face of the deep. And the Spirit of God was hovering over the face of the waters.

Advocates of this theory say "the earth was without form" should be translated "the earth *became* without form". No one denies that this is a valid possible translation of the Hebrew.

The Gap Theory was first proposed by Thomas Chalmers in 1814 as a way to reconcile evolutionary theories of an Earth that is billions of years old with chronologies derived from Genesis that indicate the Earth is more like 6000 years old. The idea is that all the missing billions of years can be fit in between Genesis 1:1 and Genesis 1:2. In Genesis 1:1 God creates the Earth. Then, billions of years later, there is some great disaster and God re-forms the Earth, and then the Bible chronologies follow from there.

They then turn to:

Revelation 21:1a Now I saw a new heaven and a new earth, for the first heaven and the first earth had passed away.

They thus find three heavens and three earths: Number one in Genesis 1:1; number two from Genesis 1:2 to Revelation 20:15; number three from Revelation 21:1 on.

In my humble opinion, theory 1 is the most likely. While the Old Testament never explicitly counts three heavens, such a count is consistent with the sky / space / God's throne usage

Theory 2 was an attempt to reconcile the Bible with the scientific theories of the day. But the science of the day was outstripped by new knowledge, the discovery of the planets Uranus and Neptune, which did not fit into the seven layers; and the discovery that the Earth is not the physical center of the universe. There's also the question of why God would have miraculously transported someone to the planet Venus – the supposed third level -- with no further explanation.

By the way, this illustrates the danger of trying to interpret God's word in light of man's latest theories rather than the other way around. When men's theories prove faulty or incomplete, your theology goes down with your outdated science. At the time you propose such an accomodationist theology, people may say, "Oh yes, here's a religion for the modern world, one that conforms to the latest scientific knowledge." But a few centuries later – or sometimes a few months later – people are laughing at your antiquated science. The same can be said for attempts to re-interpret the Bible in light of the latest fads on social or political issues.

Theory 3 also has no Biblical basis. Historically, it appears to be an attempt to "spiritualize" theory 2. By spiritualizing away the scientific theories, it saves the theory from that science being overcome by advancing knowledge. But that leaves the theory with no solid basis. The foundation proves to be made of sand, and then rather than try to build on a better foundation, advocates tried to hold the theory up with no foundation at all.

Theory 4 is built on the Gap Theory, which, like Theory 2, is an attempt to reconcile God's inspired word with the theories of fallible men. Then it tries to stretch the "new heaven and new earth" of Revelation to fit this pattern. But note that Revelation 21 says that the new heaven and earth replace the old because "the first heaven and the first earth had passed away". But according to this theory, the current heaven is the second heaven, not the first. If this theory was true, Revelation would say "the *second* heaven and the *second* earth had passed away", not the first. The new heaven of Revelation is not the third heaven, but the second.

Other things the Bible tells us about Heaven:

Jesus came from Heaven and returned to Heaven.

John 6:38 For I [Jesus] have come down from heaven, not to do My own will, but the will of Him who sent Me.

Acts 1: 10 And while they looked steadfastly toward heaven as He [Jesus] went up, behold, two men stood by them in white apparel.

Acts 7:56 and said, "Look! I see the heavens opened and the Son of Man standing at the right hand of God!"

Angels are associated with Heaven.

Genesis 22:11 But the Angel of the Lord called to him from heaven and said, "Abraham, Abraham!" So he said, "Here I am."

Luke 22:43 Then an angel appeared to Him from heaven, strengthening Him.

Angels live and/or work in Heaven.

Christians are encouraged to accumulate treasure in Heaven rather than on Earth.

Matthew 6:20-21 But lay up for yourselves treasures in heaven, where neither moth nor rust destroys and where thieves do not break in and steal. For where your treasure is, there your heart will be also.

Matthew 5: 11-12 Blessed are you when they revile and persecute you, and say all kinds of evil against you falsely for My sake. Rejoice and be exceedingly glad, for great is your reward in heaven, for so they persecuted the prophets who were before you.

1 Peter 1:3-4 3 Blessed be the God and Father of our Lord Jesus Christ, who according to His abundant mercy has begotten us again to a living hope through the resurrection of Jesus Christ from the dead, to an inheritance incorruptible and undefiled and that does not fade away, reserved in heaven for you.

Christians should keep their treasure in Heaven. God is saving a reward for us in Heaven. Our inheritance is in Heaven.

God has authority in Heaven.

Matthew 6:10 Your kingdom come. Your will be done on earth as it is in heaven.

Psalm 119:89 Forever, O Lord, Your word is settled in heaven.

While God has authority over the entire universe, including both Heaven and Earth, his will is not always carried out on Earth, because people are in rebellion against him. But his will is consistently carried out in Heaven.

So far, all of this matches popular ideas about Heaven. It's probably the sort of thing you were taught about Heaven in Sunday school.

But let's go on.

Ephesians 6:12 For we do not wrestle against flesh and blood, but against principalities, against powers, against the rulers of the darkness of this age, against spiritual hosts of wickedness in the heavenly places.

Christians must fight against forces -- apparently demons -- "in the heavenly places". If God's will is done in Heaven, then how can demons be there, demons that Christians must fight against? If we must fight them, then presumably they are not doing God's will.

Job 15:15-16 If God puts no trust in His saints, And the heavens are not pure in His sight, How much less man, who is abominable and filthy, Who drinks iniquity like water!

When he says "the heavens are not pure", in context he means morally pure: humans are evil, even saints are flawed, even heaven is not pure.

Perhaps the idea is that demons were originally angels, so they came from Heaven. They are no longer in Heaven, but they were from Heaven. A catch to this is that these verses don't say "from Heaven" but "in Heaven".

Demons may have access to Heaven.

Job 1:6 Now there was a day when the sons of God came to present themselves before the Lord, and Satan also came among them.

In Job, Satan comes before God and argues with him. Most commentators assume that this encounter took place in Heaven. The Bible doesn't specifically say where it happened. Heaven seems like a plausible place, but really, we're just guessing. If it is Heaven, maybe Satan and the demons can visit Heaven, but have no power there.

Still, the wording of Job 15 implies that these powers have their "home base" in Heaven, not just that they can occasionally visit there and that they have no power when they visit – like they have to pass through a metal detector and be disarmed.

I think the most likely possibility is to go back to the idea of multiple heavens. Perhaps God's will is consistently done in the heaven of God's throne, but demons can operate in the sky and in outer space. Note that Ephesians says that these evil spirits are in "heavenly places", not "heaven". I suspect that "heavenly places" here means outer space, as opposed to the Heaven of God's throne.

Where is the Heaven of God's throne? Is it located within the physical universe, or is it on some supernatural plane?

> Isaiah 55:9 For as the heavens are higher than the earth, So are My ways higher than your ways, And My thoughts than your thoughts.

> Job 22:12 Is not God in the height of heaven? And see the highest stars, how lofty they are!

Several places in the Bible refer to Heaven as being "high". This might be talking about the first two heavens – sky and space. The Isaiah verse above certainly could be referring to the sky as high above the Earth. But Job is talking about where God is. This might mean that Heaven is a physical place somewhere in space. Or it might be metaphorical.

Consider the physical relationship between the first heaven and the second heaven. The first heaven is above our heads, and extends up a few miles. (Scientists generally say that the "sky" becomes "space" at about 60 miles up, an admittedly arbitrary line.) So you go up a certain distance, you get to the first heaven. Go up farther still, you get to the second heaven. It's plausible to theorize that if you travelled yet farther, you would get to the third heaven. The heaven of God's throne may be a physical place within the physical universe, and not some misty spiritual realm.

Let me quickly make clear that I am not endorsing any "gods in chariots" science fiction story here, one of those theories that "the gods" are aliens from another planet and "God" is just the name of their leader, and they came to Earth, built a bunch of pyramids, and then left. I'm not suggesting anything silly like that. Rather, I'm just saying that God may have chosen to establish his throne in some natural – as opposed to supernatural – place in the universe. Just as he chose to make Jerusalem a special place in his plans, perhaps there is some place out there in space that he has made special in another way.

If the Heaven of God's throne is somewhere in outer space, do we have any clue where? Maybe one small one:

> Isaiah 14: 12-14 How you are fallen from heaven, O Lucifer, son of the morning! How you are cut down to the ground, You who weakened the nations! For you have said in your heart: 'I will ascend into heaven, I will exalt my throne above the stars of God; I will also sit on the mount of the congregation On the farthest sides of the north; I will ascend above

the heights of the clouds, I will be like the Most High.'

So when Lucifer sought to make himself like God, where did he intend to go? "above the stars" and "on the farthest sides of the north". Some commentators conclude from this that Heaven is to the north. That is, in the direction that the Earth's north pole points to, toward the star Polaris.

Some go on to point out that Leviticus 1:11 says that sacrifices to God should be made on "the north side of the altar".

Psalm 75:6-7a 6 For exaltation comes neither from the east Nor from the west nor from the south. But God is the Judge:

If it's not from east, west, or south, but from God, that implies that God is to the north.

I find the Isaiah passage interesting but not at all clear, and the other two could mean a lot of things. So in my opinion, interesting, but far from conclusive.

And here's an odd point:

Job 26:11a The pillars of heaven tremble, and are astonished at His rebuke.

Heaven has pillars? What does that mean?

You might be tempted to say this is figurative language. Except that it comes at the end of a passage that is literal or almost literal in its descriptiveness:

Job 26:7-10 He stretches out the north over empty space; He hangs the earth on nothing. He binds up the water in His thick clouds, Yet the clouds are not broken under it. He covers the face of His throne, And spreads His cloud over it. He drew a circular horizon on the face of the waters, At the boundary of light and darkness.

Notice how this whole section is made up of statements that are surprising in their technical accuracy for something written thousands of years ago. The Earth hangs over empty space: it is not on the back of a turtle or held up by Atlas. The horizon is a circle. From the surface of the Earth, the horizon looks like a straight line. From space you can see it is a circle. So perhaps the statement about the pillars of Heaven is also a description of a physical reality, and if only we knew more about the nature of the universe we would understand it.

Jeremiah 31:37 Thus says the Lord: "If heaven above can be measured, and the foundations of the earth searched out beneath, I will also cast off all the seed of Israel For all that they have done, says the Lord.

The statement is clearly rhetorical: Just as Heaven cannot be measured, so God will never abandon Israel. The point is to give assurance to Israel, and the writer takes it as a given that Heaven cannot be measured. Outer space is very big, perhaps literally infinite. Arguably, it could mean that God's habitation is very big, or that human beings do not have access to God's habitation and so cannot measure it.

Today we know that the universe is huge and that our Earth is a tiny speck in that vastness. While Christians sometimes point out off-hand comments in the Bible that demonstrate surprising (to some) scientific understanding – like I just mentioned Job's discussion of the Earth "resting on nothingness" and so on – statements about the vastness of space don't necessarily prove divine revelation. Ancient people knew that space was big. At least some ancient scholars did. About 250 BC Archimedes wrote a letter to a friend that has been called "The Sand Reckoner". In this letter he estimated the size of the universe as 10 billion stadia across. A Greek stadia was a little over 600 of our feet, so that's 6 trillion feet, or 1.1 billion miles.

Modern astronomy has found that the universe is way, way bigger than this. Our solar system alone is several times this size: The distance from our Sun to the outermost known planet, Neptune (remember Pluto got kicked out of the "planet club"), is 2.8 billion miles, so from one side of its orbit to the opposite side is 5.6 billion miles. That's just our solar system. Astronomers estimate that our galaxy contains at least 100 billion stars and is 100,000 light-years in diameter, or over 500 quadrillion miles (500,000,000,000,000,000). And our galaxy is just one among billions.

Still, even a billion miles is mind-bogglingly big.
Now here's the most surprising point.

John 3:13 No one has ascended to heaven but He who came down from heaven, that is, the Son of Man who is in heaven.

Does this mean no one else had ascended to heaven as of that time, i.e. at some point in the future people will ascend to Heaven? Or that no one ever will ascend to Heaven?

Acts 2:34 34 For David did not ascend into the heavens ...

David was certainly saved. He is described as "a man after God's own heart". But he did not go to Heaven.

I can't find any place in the Bible that says that anyone goes to Heaven when they die.

Christians are so used to the idea that the saved go to Heaven that I know that this statement will not be easily accepted. Frankly, I am very cautious about making it. How can so many Christians be wrong about this? But this is where study of scripture does seem to lead.

As I mentioned in section 1.2, the Bible says that the saved go to be with Christ, but it doesn't say that this is in Heaven. It says that the saved go to Paradise. But it doesn't say that Paradise is Heaven. (We'll discuss just what Paradise is in section 6.15.)

The Bible says that we should accumulate treasures in Heaven rather than on Earth. This might lead you to think that you go to Heaven when you die. Pile up your treasures there, and then eventually go to join them. Except the Bible never says that we will join up with these treasures in Heaven. I don't live at the bank. I've never even been to the bank that has most of my money. Mostly I communicate with them over the Internet.

Of course when Jesus talked about accumulating treasures in heaven, he wasn't talking about money or any material thing. It's not like there is a safe deposit box in Heaven in your name where God is storing gold coins or stock certificates for you. Rather, the point is that people should be more concerned about where they will spend eternity than about where they will spend their retirement. They should be more concerned about how their actions will affect their relationship with God than about how they will affect their stock portfolio. God is in Heaven, and we should be trying to please God. This is what he means by accumulating treasures in Heaven. The treasure is, to put it awkwardly, God's pleasure with us. It does not necessarily follow that we have to go to Heaven to enjoy God's favor. He could bestow his favor on us wherever we are.

Another set of verses that might have led to the idea that we will go to Heaven are those about the Kingdom of Heaven. But as I believe we showed in section 6.10, the Kingdom of Heaven is not a place, but a community of believers. The "Kingdom of Heaven" and "Heaven" are two very different things. This may sound strange but it's not really startling or even particularly unusual. This analogy may seem mundane, but: The Kingdom of Heaven is something of an organization – a church. It is not uncommon to name an organization after the place where it started or where it is headquartered. For example, the Roman Catholic Church is headquartered in Rome, but it exists all over the world. Most members have never been to Rome and never will be there. You don't have to go to Rome to be part of the Roman Catholic Church.

I find only one verse that gives any indication of Christians going to Heaven:

> Ephesians 2:4-7 But God, who is rich in mercy, because of His great love with which He loved us, even when we were dead in trespasses, made us alive together with Christ (by grace you have been saved), and raised us up together, and made us sit together in the heavenly places in Christ Jesus, that in the ages to come He might show the exceeding riches of His grace in His kindness toward us in Christ Jesus.

But note this does not say "in heaven", but "in the heavenly places". What is the difference between "heavenly places" and "heaven"? As I mentioned earlier when talking about demons operating "in the heavenly places", I suspect that this is referring to the second heaven, outer space, and not the third heaven. Perhaps in eternity we will travel through space and visit other planets, with Christ. I'll talk about this a little more in section 9.3.

So I conclude that Heaven is the place of God's throne, but it is not where the saved will spend Eternity.

All that said, in practice, in regular conversation I still talk about going to Heaven when we die. Just as, even though I know that the Earth moves around the Sun rather than the other way around, I still talk about "sunrise" and "sunset" in normal conversation.

6.12. Abraham's Bosom

Abraham's Bosom is only mentioned once in the Bible. It is in a fairly long story, the story of Lazarus and the Rich Man:

> Luke 16:19-31 "There was a certain rich man who was clothed in purple and fine linen and fared sumptuously every day. But there was a certain beggar named Lazarus, full of sores, who was laid at his gate, desiring to be fed with the crumbs which fell from the rich man's table. Moreover the dogs came and licked his sores. So it was that the beggar died, and was carried by the angels to Abraham's bosom. The rich man also died and was buried. And being in torments in Hades, he lifted up his eyes and saw Abraham afar off, and Lazarus in his bosom.
>
> "Then he cried and said, 'Father Abraham, have mercy on me, and send Lazarus that he may dip the tip of his finger in water and cool my tongue; for I am tormented in this flame.' But Abraham said, 'Son, remember that in your lifetime you received your good things, and likewise Lazarus evil things; but now he is comforted and you are tormented. And besides all this, between us and you there is a great gulf fixed, so that those who want to pass from here to you cannot, nor can those from there pass to us.'
>
> "Then he said, 'I beg you therefore, father, that you would send him to my father's house, for I have five brothers, that he may testify to them, lest they also come to this place of torment.' Abraham said to him, 'They have Moses and the prophets; let them hear them.' And he said, 'No, father Abraham; but if one goes to them from the dead, they will repent.' But he said to him, 'If they do not hear Moses and the prophets, neither will they be persuaded though one rise from the dead.'"

The gist of the story is that there are two men: a poor, saved man named Lazarus; and a rich, unsaved man whose name is not given. Both die. Lazarus goes to a good place and the rich man to a bad place.

Traditionally, this has been understood to be a true story: Jesus relates something that actually happened to two real men. Some commentators say that this is not a true story but a parable.

The argument that it is a parable generally goes like this:

- The story comes in the middle of a collection of parables, so it is probably one more in the "set".
- Jesus never says that the rich man was guilty of any sin or that Lazarus was righteous, so there is no justification why the one was in Heaven and the other in Hades.
- Several elements of the story do not make sense if taken

literally. For example, how would one drop of water relieve the rich man's suffering?

- Similarly, the rich man would not have asked for someone to come back from the dead to go to his brothers, because that would be impossible.
- If this is a literal description of eternity, then people in Heaven can see the suffering in Hell. But how could someone enjoy paradise if they could see the sufferings of their friends and family members in Hell?

Personally, I find these arguments very unconvincing.

The story does *not* come in the middle of a set of parables. It comes after a set of parables. In chapters 15 and 16 Jesus tells several parables. Then the Pharisees interrupt. Jesus replies to them by discussing the Old Testament law. In the middle of that discussion he tells this story. That doesn't prove that it's not a parable, but the context gives no evidence that it is.

The fact that Jesus did not explicitly say that Lazarus was saved and the rich man was unsaved: So what? That's implied. Why would he need to spell it out? If someone tells you a story and says that a certain person is in prison, it isn't necessary to say that he was convicted of a crime. You would take that for granted. It would only be necessary to spell it out if someone was in prison and had *not* been convicted of any crime. We make these sort of assumptions all the time when relating a story. If I tell someone that I drove to the grocery store, I don't normally first explain that I own a car, that there was sufficient gas in my car to make the trip, that I knew how to get there, and so on. That's all implied by the fact that I said I drove there.

One drop of water: People who are in difficult situations often talk about wanting some minimal relief. I've had times when I've been sick and I've said things like, "Oh, if the pain would just stop for five minutes!" How many of us in some disagreement have said, "Would you just give me an inch?!" There is nothing surprising about such a request. It's the sort of thing people say all the time.

Sending a messenger from the dead: Who says that is impossible, AND so what? If God had wanted to bring someone back from the dead to speak to this man's brothers, who is to say that he could not have done that? Indeed, within a few years after Jesus told this story, God *did* bring someone back from the dead to warn people about the dangers of Hell: the same Jesus who told this story. (And just as many people do not listen to Moses and the prophets, they do not listen to Jesus.) Even if we agree that God wouldn't have brought someone back from the dead specifically to speak to this man's brothers, he didn't necessarily know that. Even if he did know it, he could still have asked out of desperation.

See suffering: The story doesn't say that people in Heaven can see the suffering in Hades. Maybe Abraham could see it. There's no mention that Lazarus saw the suffering in Hades. But in any case, nowhere does the Bible say that people in Heaven can't see the suffering in Hell. That's a speculation that people have come up with to explain an admittedly difficult problem. More about this in section 8.10. For our purposes here, though: You cannot assume that you are right on one debated, controversial point and then use that as an argument to prove another debated, controversial point.

There are a number of reasons to think this is not a parable.

The Bible never refers to this story as a parable. That's not conclusive, as there are a number of passages that are pretty obviously parables that are not explicitly labeled as such.

This story gives specific names of several people: Lazarus, Moses, and Abraham; and one place, Hades. If this is a parable, than Lazarus is apparently a fictional character, while Moses and Abraham are clearly real people. If this is a parable, it is the only parable Jesus told in which he gave names to the characters, and also the only parable to mention real people. In all of the undisputed parables, Jesus refers to the characters only by descriptions, like "a certain man", "a landowner", and "the older brother", rather than giving them names. It would also be a bit odd to mix real people with fictional characters, though I suppose not impossible. (Some atheists might not believe that Moses and Abraham were real people, but Jesus clearly did, and the question is whether Jesus believed he was telling a true story versus a parable.)

But most important, the whole point of the parables is that they are analogies. They use a mundane, earthly situation to explain something spiritual. Jesus regularly says, "The Kingdom of Heaven is like a mustard seed" and the like. He uses a farmer planting seed as a symbol for preaching the Gospel. He uses a business owner paying his employees as a symbol for God rewarding those who believe in him.

Etc. When he explains a parable, each item and each event in the parable corresponds to an item or event in the real world. For example, when Jesus explains the Parable of the Tares:

> Matthew 13:37-39 He answered and said to them: "He who sows the good seed is the Son of Man. The field is the world, the good seeds are the sons of the kingdom, but the tares are the sons of the wicked one. The enemy who sowed them is the devil, the harvest is the end of the age, and the reapers are the angels.

Each parable is a detailed analogy.

Now consider the story of Lazarus and the Rich Man. What is the analogy? He does not say "Paradise and Hades are like ..." and then compare them to routine Earthly things. He starts with Hades. There is no comparison or symbol.

That is, the parables all use fictional people and places to represent real people and places. A landowner represents God, wheat represents the saved, etc. So if this is a parable, then Lazarus, the rich man, and Abraham must all be fictional characters, and Hades and the place where Lazarus is must be fictional places. So who or what does Abraham represent in real life? Who or what does "Hades" represent in real life? If Jesus believes that Hades is a fictional place, why does he refer to it other times as if it was real? Etc. The story makes no sense as a parable. It makes perfect sense as a true story. It is not a pleasant true story. Maybe you wish it wasn't a true story. But wishing does not make it so.

So working from the conclusion that this is a literal story and not a parable, what does it tell us about Abraham's Bosom?

Many Christian commentators talk about "Abraham's Bosom" as the name of a place. But this isn't really a name. As you may know, "bosom" is a rather obsolete word meaning "chest". Some English translations use the more modern phrase, "Abraham's side". So all that the reference to "Abraham's Bosom" means is that Lazarus was standing near Abraham, possibly that Abraham had an arm around him. Just what is this place that Lazarus goes to?

The most common reading is that Lazarus is in Heaven. But note that the text says nothing about Heaven. As we discussed in section 6.11, nowhere does the Bible say that people go to Heaven when they die. There is no evidence that Lazarus is in Heaven.

Back in section 6.1 we discussed the theory that the souls of the saved reside temporarily in a pleasant part of Sheol/Hades. Many commentators connect Abraham's Bosom with the pleasant part of Hades under this theory. At the time Jesus tells the story, he has, of course, not yet been crucified and resurrected, so by this theory, no one could yet go to Heaven. So Lazarus must be in this temporary waiting area.

An objection to this theory is that Jesus contrasts the rich man being in Hades with Lazarus being in Abraham's Bosom. If Lazarus is in Hades – not the same place that the rich man is, but another part of Hades – wouldn't this be an odd wording? Like saying, "Bob was in France, and his brother was far away in Paris."

One resolution to this is to note that Jesus doesn't just say that the rich man was in Hades, but rather, "in torments in Hades". Perhaps "torments" is a description of where he is and not of his condition. That is, perhaps what Jesus is saying is that the rich man is in the torments part of Hades while Lazarus is in the Abraham's Bosom part of Hades. Then the statement that the two are far apart is quite natural.

Some theologians therefore calls the unpleasant part of Hades "Torments". The pleasant part is variously called "Abraham's Bosom", "Bliss", and "Paradise". (We'll talk about Paradise more in section 6.15.)

6.13. New Heaven and New Earth

The Bible makes several references to a "new Heaven" and a "new Earth". Unlike most of the other words for places in Eternity that we have been discussing, it is not so easy to count the references to a new Heaven and Earth because we're talking about a descriptive phrase rather than a name. There is more than one way to say "new", and not every place that uses the words "new" and "Earth" in the same verse necessarily means the same thing.

Regardless, there are several places in the Bible that describe a new Heaven and Earth.

The Earth that we live on today will not exist forever.

Psalm 102:25-26 Long ago You established the earth, and the heavens are the work of Your hands. They will perish, but You will endure; all of them will wear out like clothing. You will change them like a garment, and they will pass away.

Matthew 24:35 Heaven and earth will pass away, but My words will never pass away.

At some point the Earth will be destroyed. How will it happen?

2 Peter 3:10 But the day of the Lord will come as a thief in the night, in which the heavens will pass away with a great noise, and the elements will melt with fervent heat; both the earth and the works that are in it will be burned up.

The Greek word translated "elements" here is "stoicheion". It means an indivisible unit, and was often used for things like letters of the alphabet. It is the same word that Plato used for elements in the sense of atoms. That is, it means "element" in the same sense that modern chemists talk about chemical elements.

Perhaps I should explain that the Greeks had theories about matter being made up of atoms that were strikingly similar to modern theories, at least in their essence. The Greeks got there more by logic than by experiment. Suppose, they said, that you cut something in half. Aristotle used cheese as an example. You get two smaller pieces of cheese. Suppose you cut one of those in half. You get yet smaller pieces of cheese. Can you keep doing this forever, getting smaller and smaller pieces of cheese? Or is there some point at which you have the smallest possible piece of cheese, and if you cut that in half, you now have ... something else. They theorized that in fact there was a smallest possible piece of anything, and that if you were then able to cut this thing into yet smaller pieces, you would find what they called "atoms". From there they considered fire. When you burn a piece of wood, for example, you get fire and ash. What if fire was one of these atoms? Perhaps wood is made up of several atoms, one of which is fire. When you remove the fire, the remaining atoms make ash.

This isn't quite how modern chemists see it, but the concept is the same: everything is made up of atoms, and these atoms can be re-arranged through chemical reactions to make other things.

So the very elements, the atoms, making up the Earth will be destroyed. Peter is not saying that there would be anything as trivial as a big hurricane or an earthquake. He was saying that the entire planet will be completely destroyed.

Then what?

Revelation 21:1 Then I saw a new heaven and a new earth, for the first heaven and the first earth had passed away, and the sea no longer existed.

After the Earth is destroyed, John, the writer of Revelation, is shown a new Earth.

Many commentators describe this as the Earth being reformed or remodeled. But that does not really match the description. The Earth is not simply dusted off and cleaned up. It is burned to a cinder. Then John is shown a new Earth.

We may need a new Earth because the old Earth has been so badly damaged. There are centuries of mismanagement of what God has given us, especially pollution and war. God's final judgments on the Earth as described in Revelation do more damage. The Earth may simply be ruined at this point.

John says that the new Earth has no oceans. He does not elaborate on this, so it is not clear if this is significant or if it's simply a statement of fact. It does tell us that the new Earth is not a photocopy of the current Earth. If there are no oceans, then there can't be a North America and Europe and Asia and so on, as the continents are defined by their boundaries with the oceans.

What does it mean when it says that the old heaven is destroyed and John sees a new heaven? This brings us back to the discussion of "three heavens": sky, space, and God's abode.

This might mean that the sky is also destroyed. If the Earth is burned up, the sky would surely go with it. A new Earth would have its own sky.

It might mean that the entire physical universe is destroyed and a new one created to replace it.

It seems unlikely that it means that God's abode is destroyed and replaced. Destroying the Earth would inevitably destroy the sky. We can comprehend God destroying the entire physical universe, including the Earth. But it's difficult to see how the destruction of the Earth would be connected to the destruction of God's abode. Maybe, but it doesn't sound as logical as other theories.

Maybe I'm stretching here, but I think that it means that the new Earth is in a different place in space. There is a new Earth, and from it one sees different stars, planets, and constellations, i.e. new heavens.

Note that the Bible does not say that God creates the new Earth at this time, but simply that John saw a new Earth. This may mean that the new Earth already existed, and John is simply shown it at this time. It may exist now; it may have been created during the initial creation week, and preserved for when it was needed. Or it may be new in the sense that it is created at that time.

6.14. New Jerusalem

New Jerusalem is only mentioned once in the Bible, in chapters 21 and 22 of Revelation. But unlike many of the places that we have discussed, we are given a rather extensive description. For most of the places in Eternity, we are given only fleeting, off-hand references. But New Jerusalem is described in some detail.

> Revelation 21:9-22:5 [An angel] came to me and talked with me, saying, "Come, I will show you the bride, the Lamb's wife." And he carried me away in the Spirit to a great and high mountain, and showed me the great city, the holy Jerusalem, descending out of heaven from God, having the glory of God. Her light was like a most precious stone, like a jasper stone, clear as crystal. Also she had a great and high wall with twelve gates, and twelve angels at the gates, and names written on them, which are the names of the twelve tribes of the children of Israel ...

> Now the wall of the city had twelve foundations, and on them were the names of the twelve apostles of the Lamb. And he who talked with me had a gold reed to measure the city, its gates, and its wall. The city is laid out as a square; its length is as great as its breadth. And he measured the city with the reed: twelve thousand furlongs. Its length, breadth, and height are equal. Then he measured its wall: one hundred and forty-four cubits, according to the measure of a man, that is, of an angel. The construction of its wall was of jasper; and the city was pure gold, like clear glass. The foundations of the wall of the city were adorned with all kinds of precious stones. ... The twelve gates were twelve pearls: each individual gate was of one pearl. And the street of the city was pure gold, like transparent glass.

> But I saw no temple in it, for the Lord God Almighty and the Lamb are its temple. The city had no need of the sun or of the moon to shine in it, for the glory of God illuminated it. The Lamb is its light. And the nations of those who are saved shall walk in its light, and the kings of the earth bring their glory and honor into it. Its gates shall not be shut at all by day (there shall be no night there). And they shall bring the glory and the honor of the nations into it. But there shall by no means enter it anything

that defiles, or causes an abomination or a lie, but only those who are written in the Lamb's Book of Life.

And he showed me a pure river of water of life, clear as crystal, proceeding from the throne of God and of the Lamb. In the middle of its street, and on either side of the river, was the tree of life, which bore twelve fruits, each tree yielding its fruit every month. The leaves of the tree were for the healing of the nations. And there shall be no more curse, but the throne of God and of the Lamb shall be in it, and His servants shall serve Him. They shall see His face, and His name shall be on their foreheads. There shall be no night there: They need no lamp nor light of the sun, for the Lord God gives them light. And they shall reign forever and ever.

Well, there's a lot there.

New Jerusalem is introduced as "the bride, the lamb's wife". There are a number of places in the Bible that refer to the church as the "bride of Christ".

2 Corinthians 11:2 For I am jealous for you with godly jealousy. For I have betrothed you to one husband, that I may present you as a chaste virgin to Christ.

Similarly, see Ephesians 5:25-27, John 3:29, Mathew 25, etc.
God also describes himself as the husband of Israel.

Isaiah 54:5 For your Maker is your husband, The Lord of hosts is His name; And your Redeemer is the Holy One of Israel; He is called the God of the whole earth.

The gates of New Jerusalem are named after the twelve tribes of Israel. The foundations are named after the twelve apostles. New Jerusalem is the Church and Israel. That is, it is both the Old Testament saved and the New Testament saved.

In New Jerusalem, God will live with men. There is no more death; no more sorrow; no more pain. New Jerusalem has pearly gates and streets of gold.

This sounds a lot like the traditional picture of Heaven. It is from Revelation's description of New Jerusalem that we get a lot of our ideas about Heaven.

But nowhere does the Bible say that New Jerusalem is Heaven.

There are at least two very specific reasons to say that New Jerusalem is not Heaven.

Revelation 21:2 describes New Jerusalem "coming down out of Heaven". If New Jerusalem is coming out of Heaven, than it cannot be Heaven: it can't come out of itself.

In section 8.18 we'll discuss the temple in Heaven. But for our purposes here: Revelation 11:19 says that there is a temple in Heaven. Revelation 21:22 says that there is no temple in the New Jerusalem. Therefore, they cannot be the same place.

So several times now I've said that the Bible does not say that the saved spend Eternity in Heaven. Where does it say that they spend Eternity? Now we've finally gotten to the answer: in New Jerusalem.

When discussing other places in Eternity, we've noted when the Bible gives a physical description. You may have noticed that these descriptions have been pretty sparse and vague. When it comes to New Jerusalem the Bible tells us a number of things about its physical nature and location.

We're told that the base of New Jerusalem is a square, but we are not given any description of the shape in the third dimension. Some suppose that if the base is a perfect square, the sides are probably also squares so that New Jerusalem is a cube. Others say it is a pyramid. I don't see anything in the text to indicate that, and the only arguments I've heard for it are pretty vague, like "it must be a pyramid because a pyramid is the perfect shape". As we are specifically told the shape of the base but not of the third dimension, I suspect that the shape is irregular.

New Jerusalem has a base that is a square 12,000 furlongs on each side. The Greek says 12,000 stadia. It is also 12,000 stadia tall. A Greek stadia was 600 feet, and their "foot" was slightly longer than ours, so a stadia was probably about 607 of our feet. So 12,000 stadia is about 1400 of our modern miles. Some sources say 1500 miles. But let's be conservative and go with 1400.

Think about how big this is. 1400 miles square is 1,960,000 square miles. The entire United States is 3,800,000 square miles. So New Jerusalem would cover over half of the United States.

To put it in terms that John would think of when he was writing Revelation: The Roman Empire was about 2 million square miles. New Jerusalem was about the same size as his entire home nation.

There are only six countries in the world today larger than New Jerusalem: Russia, Canada, China, the U.S., Brazil, and Australia. For the people of any other nation, New Jerusalem is larger than their entire country.

The Moon is 2160 miles in diameter. If New Jerusalem was on the Moon, it would cover 2/3 of the width as seen from Earth. The square base of New Jerusalem would be over half the size of the disc of the Moon.

Even this understates the size. New Jerusalem is not just 2 million square miles. It is also 1400 miles tall. It seems unlikely that it is one giant room with a 1400 mile high ceiling. The interior is probably divided into levels or floors, like tall buildings on Earth. Suppose, just for the sake of argument, that each level has a 100 foot ceiling. 1400 miles divided by 100 feet gives 73,920 stories. If it is in fact a cube, than that means 73,920 stories each with a floor space of 1,960,000 miles. Multiplying 1,960,000 square miles by 73,920 stories gives a total floor space of over 144 billion square miles. The total surface area of the Earth, including land, seas, and oceans, is 200 million square miles. The floor space of New Jerusalem could be over 700 times the entire surface area of the Earth.

This place is big.

Of course if it is to be the home of all the saved, it has to be big. How many saved people have lived through all of history? No one knows. Even if we knew, we don't know how many more people will be saved in the future. According to the Pew Research Center, there were 2.1 billion Christians in the world in 2010. (http://www.pewforum.org/2011/12/19/global-christianity-exec/) Most of these are only nominal Christians, that is, people who will check the box for "Christian" when asked their religion on a census form, but who don't really believe the Bible and have not committed their lives to Christ. I've seen estimates of the total number of people who have ever lived ranging from 6 billion to over 100 billion. (The 6 billion estimate was made at a time when world population was 3 billion, so adding in people born since then, say 10 billion.) I think that range makes clear that no one really knows. You have to make all sorts of guesses about how long people in the past lived, how many children died in infancy, at what age people had children, etc. Evolutionists estimate higher than creationists because they suppose many more generations of people. I just did some calculations and came up with an estimate of 70 billion, not counting infant deaths. Let's take the high end and suppose 100 billion. And let's suppose that 25% of all those people were saved – also probably a very high estimate. That would give 25 billion saved since the creation of the world. Even with this high estimate, New Jerusalem will have less than 0.2 people per square mile. Do you think Wyoming is sparsely populated? Wyoming has 6 people per square mile. That's 30 times as crowded as New Jerusalem. There's plenty of room for the saved of future generations.

Most commentators read Revelation 21:2, saying that John saw New Jerusalem "coming down out of Heaven", as meaning that it descends from Heaven and lands on the Earth. But where would such a thing land? If it landed in the United States, it would crush half the country. Mount Everest is six miles high; New Jerusalem is 1400 miles. This is not something that can just sit on the ground: it would rise far, far above the surface, many times farther than the tallest mountains. How much would something this size weigh? It might well throw the Earth out of balance, disrupting its rotation.

It is just not practical for the New Jerusalem to land. I think that when John said he saw it coming down out of Heaven, he meant that it was in orbit, like a gigantic space station or an artificial moon. Note that by this point in John's narrative the Earth has been destroyed, so it's orbiting the New Earth, not our current Earth. I'm sorry if this sounds like a science fiction story rather than a Bible study, but that's the only thing I see that makes sense.

There are a number of details to the description. But almost all of them are puzzling, perhaps more puzzling the more we think about them.

"The nations of those who are saved shall walk in its light." The light here is probably symbolic. The saved shall live their lives in accordance with the will of God as preached from this city. It's barely possible that the light is literal. If New Jerusalem is in orbit, and it is as big as we discussed above, it would give light on the (new) Earth below just as the Moon gives light to our Earth. Note that John says, "Her light was like a most precious stone, like a jasper stone, clear as crystal." New Jerusalem does give off light. So the nations of the Earth could literally "walk in its light".

"The leaves of the tree were for the healing of nations". This sounds like it means that the leaves are used as medicine or to make medicine. We generally think that there is no disease in Eternity. So why would anyone need medicine? Does this mean there is disease but it is quickly cured? That ingesting the leaves prevents disease? I don't know.

"The kings of the earth bring their glory and honor into it." What does this mean? What is the "glory" and "honor" that they bring? I'd guess that this means that they bring samples of their greatest achievements: their best art, literature, artifacts, perhaps tokens of other sorts of accomplishments.

Note that there are still nations and kings in Eternity.

We're also told that the gates are always open. So people are coming and going from New Jerusalem all the time. The saved do not go to New Jerusalem and just stay there.

If the gates are always open, then why have gates at all? (Like, if the convenience store is open 24 hours a day, 7 days a week, why do they have locks on the doors?) "Open" here might mean "unlocked" rather than literally the doors always being open. Or perhaps by "gates" it just means that there are openings in the walls. If New Jerusalem is indeed in orbit, the gates might be airlocks, in which case they constantly open and close. Or do we need air in Eternity?

The wall is 144 cubits. This is about 216 feet. Curiously, we are not told exactly what dimension of the wall is 216 feet. Is it 216 feet high? 216 feet thick? Or what?

It seems very unlikely that it means 216 feet long. It is 1400 times 4 miles around the city, or 5600 miles. A wall that covered only 216 feet of that length would be barely worth mentioning.

The city is 1400 miles tall, so a 216 foot wall would only go a very short way up. It's possible that it means that there is a wall that is 216 feet tall that goes around the base and then there are various buildings that rise much higher.

Most likely it means that the wall is 216 feet thick. That's a very thick wall, but remember how big the city is. This is a tiny percentage of the size of the city. Given the size of this thing, it might need very strong walls to give it structural integrity.

Each of the foundations of the city is a different jewel. There is no further explanation of this. Does each jewel have some symbolic significance? If so, this isn't explained anywhere. I cannot find anything in the Bible that says "emeralds represent charity" or any such thing, directly or indirectly.

Perhaps they have some practical purpose. Plausible, but I have no idea what that might be.

Maybe they are simply to be pretty. That may sound like I'm trivializing Scripture, but isn't it plausible that God would create beauty for its own sake?

The gates are each made of a single pearl. This is where people get the idea that Heaven has "pearly gates". Again, whether this has symbolic significance, a practical purpose, or is simply to be pretty, is hard to say.

Pearls are produced inside clams and other mollusks. The largest pearl ever found is known as the Pearl of Lao Tzu. It is a little under 9 ½ inches in diameter and weighs 14 pounds. This is a very big pearl, but it would make a very small gate for a city. Where do the pearls for the gates of New Jerusalem come from? Will God create giant clams somewhere? That sounds like a joke. I tend to think that God will simply miraculously create giant pearls. As miracles go, that's probably a lot easier than making the Sun stand still or creating a world. Perhaps there's more of a story there.

We are told that "the street" is pure gold. When you read this in English it sounds like there is only one street in New Jerusalem. But it probably doesn't mean that. The word translated "street" here is the Greek word "plateia". It can mean a broad main street or a square, as in a town square. It is often used in Greece today to refer to a town square or other large open paved area. So this probably means that there is some large central square in New Jerusalem or a broad main street that is paved with gold.

There are two references to gold that is clear or transparent. But gold is not transparent. What can this mean? Some commentators say that by "transparent" it really means shiny or sparkling. But the Greek word is "diaphanes", which simply cannot mean shiny: It means "see-through". It doesn't necessarily mean totally transparent, it is used to refer to a thin cloth, for example. But gold is not see-through in any sense.

Furthermore, one of the descriptions is the surface of a street or square. Gold is a very soft metal. It would not be suitable for a street.

One possibility is that John doesn't mean the chemical element gold, atomic number 79. Perhaps he simply means something that is the color gold. In that case it could be anything, including something transparent.

Perhaps John doesn't mean a solid block of gold metal, but rather some other substance with gold embedded in it. But again we run into trouble: the text emphasizes "pure gold", which would seem to contradict the idea of gold mixed with something else. Perhaps it means that the embedded gold is pure.

I think the simplest explanation is that John is describing something unfamiliar. He saw a material that looked like gold but that was transparent, so that's how he describes it.

There is no need for the sun to shine there, because God provides light. This is discussed twice, which would seem to indicate that it's important. It does not mean some sort of artificial light, because we are told that lamps are not needed either. The simplest reading would seem to be that God miraculously provides light. But there's no clue to the mechanism.

A side ramble: The foundations are named after the twelve apostles. Is the twelfth name Judas? Probably not. Is number twelve Matthias? (Acts 1:15-26) Some have suggested that God's choice for the apostle to replace Judas was Paul.

So as you can see, there are a number of details, but many of them are tantalizingly unclear. Exactly what do all these details mean?

There are some interesting parallels between the Garden of Eden and the New Jerusalem. There are too many to just be a coincidence.

Eden	New Jerusalem
God is present with men	God is present with men
source of four rivers	River of Life
Tree of Life at center of garden	Tree of Life along street
beginning of curse	no more curse
angel guards entrance	angels at gates
dominion over Earth	reign with Christ

Of course there is one very stark contrast: Eden was a garden, while New Jerusalem is a city. Perhaps New Jerusalem is what Eden was supposed to become: God placed people in a garden, but he told them to have dominion over the world. We were supposed to build and create – perhaps to build and create a great city like New Jerusalem.

The name "New Jerusalem" does not appear anywhere in the Bible other than Revelation. But there may be some other references to it by other names, or without giving a specific name.

> Hebrews 11:13,16 These all died in faith, not having received the promises, but having seen them afar off were assured of them, embraced them and confessed that they were strangers and pilgrims on the earth. ... But now they desire a better, that is, a heavenly country. Therefore God is not ashamed to be called their God, for He has prepared a city for them.

> Hebrews 12:22-23 But you have come to Mount Zion and to the city of the living God, the heavenly Jerusalem, to an innumerable company of angels, to the general assembly and church of the firstborn who are registered in heaven, to God the Judge of all, to the spirits of just men made perfect ...

I think it's likely these verses are talking about New Jerusalem.

"Zion" was another name for Jerusalem. King David conquered the city of Jerusalem from another nation, the Jebusites. 2 Samuel 5:7 describes this battle and calls the city, or a Jebusite fort near or within the city, "Zion". David renamed the city "the City of David", but this name did not appear to catch on, and by the end of the chapter it is called "Jerusalem". (Besides Zion, City of David, and Jerusalem, people also called this city Salem and Jebus in earlier times.)

The hill within Jerusalem on which Solomon's Temple was built came to be called "Mount Zion". Zion is thus used as a poetic name for Jerusalem in general, for the temple hill more specifically, and by extension for God's presence among the Jews. Thus the idea that Zion or Mount Zion might be another name for New Jerusalem is not very much of a stretch. As Zion is another name for Jerusalem to begin with, all we're missing is the word "New". After Jerusalem was conquered by the Babylonians, the word Zion quickly took on a spiritual meaning, so adding a qualifying word like "new" may have seemed unnecessary.

Some Jews and Christians use the word Zion as another name for Heaven, that is, of the place where the saved will spend Eternity. Arguably, in this book I should have included it as one of the places in Eternity. But most of the references to Zion in the Bible are referring to the earthly city of Jerusalem. It is difficult to sort them out, and it didn't seem to add much to the conversation.

None of these other references to an eternal Zion or to New Jerusalem seem to really add any information about the place itself.

> Psalm 46:4-6 There is a river whose streams shall make glad the city of God, The holy place of the tabernacle of the Most High. God is in the midst of her, she shall not be moved; God shall help her, just at the break of dawn. The nations raged, the kingdoms were moved; He uttered His voice, the earth melted.

This sounds like New Jerusalem in several ways: it's a city, God lives there with his people, and it has a river. There's also the mention of "the earth melted", which sounds like the description of the destruction of the Earth and the creation of the new Earth, though that isn't necessarily literal – he may just be emphasizing the power of God's word.

> John 14:2-3 In My Father's house are many mansions; if it were not so, I would have told you. I go to prepare a place for you. And if I go and prepare a place for you, I will come again and receive you to Myself; that where I am, there you may be also.

The word translated "mansions" here is a general word for "living places". Some translations say "in my Father's house are many rooms".

In ancient Israel, when a couple was to be married, the groom was supposed to build or prepare a room or apartment attached to his father's house where the couple would spend at least the first seven days of their marriage. Many commentators connect Jesus statement here to this traditional wedding chamber.

Unlike a wedding where there is only one bride (normally, anyway), in the case of the Church there are many individuals, so Jesus is preparing "many" places. So the sense conveyed here is that the Church will live in a place where there are many "apartments" of some kind.

This fits the idea of the New Jerusalem. Jesus is preparing a great city where there will be many homes or apartments for all the saved.

But remember again how big this place is. These don't have to be tiny apartments like in a crowded Earthly city. They may all be penthouse suites, with plenty of room left over for parks and recreation centers!

6.15. Paradise

The word "Paradise" is used in three places in the New Testament. It is not used in the Old Testament. Paradise is the English translation of the Greek word "paradeison".

We often talk about Eden as a "paradise", but the Bible does not use the word to describe Eden.

The first reference is when Jesus was on the cross:

> Luke 23:39-43 Then one of the criminals who were hanged blasphemed Him, saying, "If You are the Christ, save Yourself and us." But the other, answering, rebuked him, saying, "Do you not even fear God, seeing you are under the same condemnation? And we indeed justly, for we receive the due reward of our deeds; but this Man has done nothing wrong." Then he said to Jesus, "Lord, remember me when You come into Your kingdom." And Jesus said to him, "Assuredly, I say to you, today you will be with Me in Paradise."

So the saved go to Paradise when they die. Jesus will be there with us.

By the way, this also tells us that salvation is by grace and not by works. The thief admits that he is guilty of many sins and deserves death. He will die there on the cross within a few hours so even if there were some good deeds he could do to make up for his sins, he won't have a chance to do them. And yet Jesus tells him that he is among the saved.

The second reference we already discussed in a different context, in section 6.11 on Heaven.

> 2 Corinthians 12:2-4 I know a man in Christ who fourteen years ago — whether in the body I do not know, or whether out of the body I do not know, God knows — such a one was caught up to the third heaven. And I know such a man — whether in the body or out of the body I do not know, God knows — how he was caught up into Paradise ...

So this man was transported to the third Heaven, and this man was transported to Paradise. Is this two places or one? There's a parallel structure here, "caught up to the third heaven … caught up into Paradise". That could mean this is two ways of saying the same thing, or it could mean two similar things.

Revelation 2:7b To him who overcomes I will give to eat from the tree of life, which is in the midst of the Paradise of God.

So the tree of life is in Paradise. That's interesting of itself. But it may give another important clue. Later in the book of Revelation, in the description of the New Jerusalem (section 6.14), we are told:

Revelation 22:2a In the middle of its street, and on either side of the river, was the tree of life.

So the tree of life is in Paradise, and the tree of life is in New Jerusalem. Are there two trees of life? Or is Paradise another name for New Jerusalem?

So here's my theory. Admittedly, the evidence is thin, but it does hang together:

Paradise is another name for New Jerusalem. Both names are associated with the tree of life. Both places are places where Jesus is present. Most important, both names are described as places where the saved spend Eternity. And finally, recall that John saw a vision of the future in which he sees the New Jerusalem "descending out of heaven". The person in 2 Corinthians 12 saw Paradise in Heaven. If at some time in the future New Jerusalem will descend from Heaven, that implies that now it is in Heaven. So that part is consistent.

Unlike some of the place names that people say are two names for the same place, there is nothing in the Bible that clearly says these are two different places. Like Hades and the Lake of Fire can't be the same place, because we are told that Hades is thrown into the Lake of Fire and destroyed. And New Jerusalem can't be Heaven because there's a temple in Heaven and there is no temple in New Jerusalem. There's no such conflict with New Jerusalem and Paradise. Of course that doesn't prove that they're the same. Maybe such a negative just isn't mentioned.

"New Jerusalem" is a name while "Paradise" is a description, so there's nothing particularly odd about applying both terms to the same place.

It's possible that these are two different places and the saved go to both of them. Maybe we go to one for a period of time and then to the other. Or maybe they are two places that the saved visit, going back and forth. The gates of New Jerusalem are always open, so it's not like we'll be locked in.

On the other hand, some commentators say that there are two places called Paradise: New Jerusalem and also the pleasant part of Sheol/Hades. This seems unlikely to me: why would God use one name for two places? Perhaps it is not intended to be a name but rather a description.

All told, I think it is likely that New Jerusalem is Paradise. This is a long way from proof, but it's plausible.

6.16. Limbo

"Limbo" comes from the Latin word "limbus", meaning "edge". The word is not found in the Bible. It was invented by Catholic theologians. Just because the word is not found in the Bible doesn't necessarily mean it's not real: People routinely invent words for an idea or a theory. Bible scholars have invented many words for ideas where the idea is in the Bible but the word is not, like "trinity" and "Mosaic law".

Catholic theologians talk of two Limbos: Limbo of the Fathers and Limbo of the Infants. Neither is official Church doctrine, but it is a common theory among Catholics.

The theory of the Limbo of the Fathers is that before Christ died, no one could go to Heaven, because no one's sins had yet been paid for. So the righteous dead had to go to a temporary place, a "waiting room", until Christ could come for them. Note we discussed essentially the same theory in section 6.1, Sheol, without using the term Limbo. So many Protestants hold to a similar theory, they just call it Sheol instead of Limbo of the Fathers. (See 6.1 for more discussion of this theory.)

The theory of Limbo of the Infants is that it is a place for the souls of children who die before they are old enough to know right from wrong and so make an informed decision about accepting Christ. The idea is that a just God would not send them to Hell because they have not knowingly committed any sins, their sins are in ignorance. But he also cannot admit them to Heaven because they have not accepted Christ. So there must be some other place to send them. Thus, Limbo.

The scriptural justification for this idea is thin. It is primarily the result of philosophical speculation.

There are some Bible verses that might mean that children are in a special category.

> Deuteronomy 1:39 Moreover your little ones and your children, who you say will be victims, who today have no knowledge of good and evil, they shall go in there; to them I will give it, and they shall possess it.

The key words here being that children "have no knowledge of good and evil". I'm not saying this verse is talking about Eternity: it's not, it's talking about the people of Israel taking the land of Palestine. I'm just making the point that the Bible does seem to put children who are not old enough to know right from wrong in a special category.

When Job is describing his desperate situation, he says:

> Job 3:16-17 Or why was I not hidden like a stillborn child, Like infants who never saw light? There the wicked cease from troubling, And there the weary are at rest.

So stillborn children are "at rest". Does this mean in Heaven? In Limbo?

When David and Bathsheba's first son dies, David says:

> 2 Samuel 12:22 And he said, "While the child was alive, I fasted and wept; for I said, 'Who can tell whether the Lord will be gracious to me, that the child may live?' But now he is dead; why should I fast? Can I bring him back again? I shall go to him, but he shall not return to me."

David believed that he and his dead baby would eventually be re-united in Eternity. This indicates a special status for children but not a separate Limbo. We should bear in mind that the Bible says that David said this, not that the statement itself is true.

On the other hand, some verses seem to indicate that children have no special dispensation, and an unsaved child suffers the same fate as an unsaved adult:

> Psalm 51:5 Behold, I was brought forth in iniquity, And in sin my mother

conceived me.

Psalm 58:3 The wicked are estranged from the womb; They go astray as soon as they are born, speaking lies.

Proverbs 20:11 Even a child is known by his deeds, whether what he does is pure and right.

Many Protestants believe that children who are not old enough to understand right and wrong are "automatically" saved and go to Heaven. This is not quite the same as the Catholic idea of Limbo. Protestants are saying that adults who accept Christ and children who die in ignorance go to the same place. Catholics are saying that neither go to Hell but they go to different places.

I don't claim to know the answer to this difficult question. So I'll just leave this there.

6.17. Purgatory

Like Limbo, Purgatory is a term invented by Catholic theologians. It is not found in the Bible. And like Limbo of the Infants, it has no clear basis in any Bible verses, but rather is a place hypothesized based on philosophical reasoning.

The theory is that people who are saved don't go directly to Heaven, but first must spend some amount of time in Purgatory to be "purged" of their sins. It is an intermediate place where souls are prepared for Heaven.

Most Protestants reject the idea of Purgatory, though Anglicans, some Lutherans, and others accept it. A classic difference between Protestants and Catholics is that most Protestants believe in a doctrine of salvation purely by grace, that there is nothing a person can do to be saved except trust in Christ. Catholics believe that we must still live holy lives to earn our salvation. So from a Catholic point of view, it stands to reason that if you have sins that you have not repented and atoned for in this life, you must do something in the next life to make up for them. Hence, there must be some intermediate place where you "work off" the penalties for your sins. Hence, Purgatory.

Protestants reply that Christ has already paid the penalty for our sins, so there is no need for us to do something more to add to Christ's work, and indeed there is nothing we are capable of doing to "earn" salvation.

One of Martin Luther's key complaints about the Catholic Church that led him to breaking away was the doctrine of Purgatory, and abuses of that doctrine. He particularly objected to the idea that you could help a friend or family member be released from Purgatory sooner by giving money to the Catholic Church. Luther was especially outraged by a slogan used by Friar Johann Tetzel when soliciting contributions: "As soon as the money clinks into the money chest, the soul flies out of purgatory."

7. Maps of the Universe

The Geography of Heaven

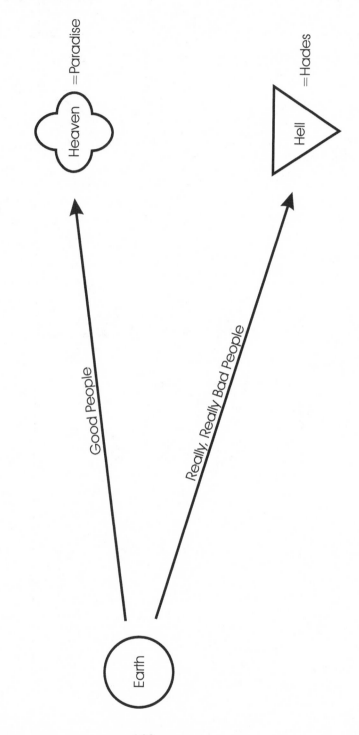

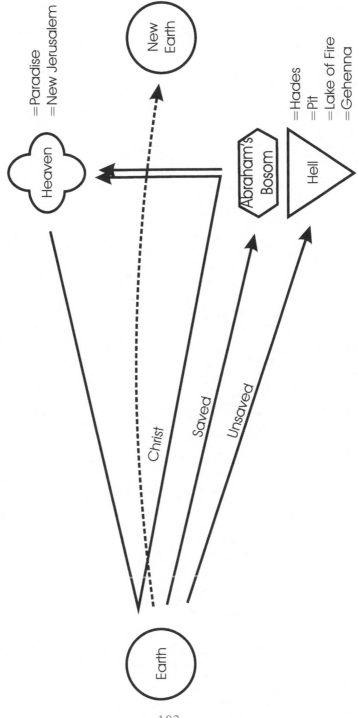

FAIRLY TYPICAL PROTESTANT VIEW

New Earth

=Paradise
=New Jerusalem

Heaven

Abraham's Bosom

Hell

=Hades
=Pit
=Lake of Fire
=Gehenna

Christ

Saved

Unsaved

Earth

The Geography of Heaven

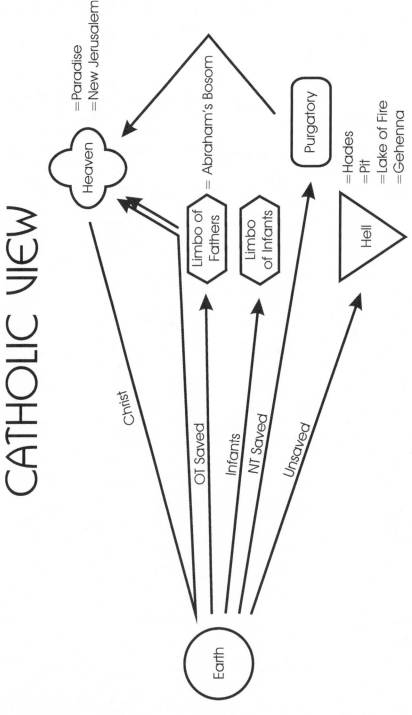

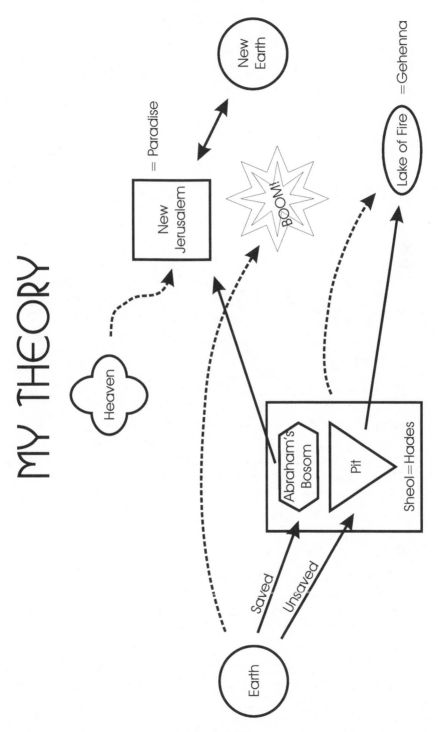

8. Places Revisited

8.1. Introduction

So now we've made the grand tour, listing all the places in Eternity that the Bible describes. We've gone through each place one by one, describing what we can learn about it, it's function and role.

Of course there is much more that can be said about each place. And there are interesting questions about Eternity that aren't specifically about one place or another.

In this section I break from the "tour" approach to revisit some places and discuss some more general questions.

8.2. What does the Devil look like?

The Devil is often pictured as having red skin, horns, and a tail, and carrying a pitchfork.

There is no such description of the Devil in the Bible, or anything remotely resembling it.

Nowhere does the Bible clearly describe what the Devil looks like.

There is something that could be taken as a physical description of the Devil in Revelation:

Revelation 12:3,9 And another sign appeared in heaven: behold, a great, fiery red dragon having seven heads and ten horns, and seven diadems on his heads. ... So the great dragon was cast out, that serpent of old, called the Devil and Satan, who deceives the whole world; he was cast to the earth, and his angels were cast out with him.

In a vision, John sees a dragon with seven heads and ten horns, and a little later we are told that this dragon is the Devil.

But this is probably not a literal description of what the Devil looks like. It comes in the middle of a section full of symbols. Just before the Devil is introduced we are told about a woman who apparently represents Israel, and after it we are told about two strange-looking "beasts" who we are clearly told are symbols for empires, and not literal monsters. Note the description begins by saying "a sign appeared in heaven" – a "sign", not a "photograph". So it is more likely that the dragon is intended to be a symbol representing attributes of the Devil, rather than a description of what he actually looks like.

In Genesis 3 we are told that the Devil appeared to Adam and Eve in Eden as a serpent. It doesn't say if this is his true, natural form, or a disguise that he took on to trick Eve.

In 2 Corinthians, Paul discusses false teachers who try to pretend they are something they are not. In the course of this discussion he writes:

2 Corinthians 11:13-14 For such are false apostles, deceitful workers, transforming themselves into apostles of Christ. And no wonder! For Satan himself transforms himself into an angel of light.

So the Devil sometimes appears to people as a beautiful angel.

And that's about all we know. Of course the Devil is a spiritual being. Perhaps he doesn't have a "physical appearance". Perhaps he has the ability to change form at will so that describing his appearance would be a meaningless statement.

8.3.   Is there literal fire in Hell?

The Bible describes Hell as a place of fire.

Matthew 18:9 And if your eye causes you to sin, pluck it out and cast it from you. It is better for you to enter into life with one eye, rather than having two eyes, to be cast into hell fire.

Matt 25:41 "Depart from Me, you cursed, into the everlasting fire prepared for the devil and his angels"

Et cetera, there are many similar verses.

Some people say that this is symbolic or figurative. God doesn't really condemn people to literally burn for eternity. Rather, this language is just intended to make clear that Hell is an unpleasant place.

They quote verses such as:

2 Peter 2:4 "For if God did not spare the angels who sinned, but cast them down to hell [Tartarus] and delivered them into chains of darkness"

Matt 25:30 "cast the unprofitable servant into the outer darkness."

That is, Hell is described as a place of darkness. But if a Hell is dark, then it cannot be filled with fire.

Furthermore, fire is often used as a symbol of the judgment of God.

Deuteronomy 4:24 For the Lord your God is a consuming fire, a jealous God.

Isaiah 30:27 Behold, the name of the Lord comes from afar, Burning with His anger, And His burden is heavy; His lips are full of indignation, And His tongue like a devouring fire.

Clearly the language here is symbolic. God's tongue is not literally fire; this is just a poetic way of describing his anger and judgment.

So, people who take this position argue, the fires of Hell are not literal either. This is just a poetic or symbolic description to indicate that Hell is a place of judgment.

There are several problems with this.

One could, I suppose, argue that it is the darkness that is figurative rather than the fire. If literal fire and literal darkness are contradictory, how do we know that it is the fire that is symbolic and not the darkness? Darkness is a symbol of ignorance and separation from God.

But I wouldn't argue that. Rather, I say that there is nothing in the text to indicate that either the darkness or the fire is symbolic.

It's not that hard to reconcile fire and darkness. When I was younger and less addicted to comfort I used to go camping. We often built campfires at night. Yes, the fire gave off light, but all around was dark. The Bible doesn't say that every square inch of Hell is fire, nor that every square inch is dark. There could be fires all around and the place still generally be dark. The fires could come and go: there could be periods of darkness and then a blast of flame. One could come up with more complex scenarios, like the fire is underground so that the ground is burning hot but there are no visible flames. Etc.

In any case, the whole point of this line of argument seems to be to argue that Hell is not the place of torment that we typically picture. They are trying to say that it is not a place of constant torture, but only a place where people are deprived of the joy of God's presence. We'll get back to this point in section 8.5, but that's a big "only". Regardless of the exact nature of Hell, the Bible makes clear that it is an extremely unpleasant place to be.

Revelation 14:10b-11a He shall be tormented with fire and brimstone in the presence of the holy angels and in the presence of the Lamb. And the smoke of their torment ascends forever and ever; and they have no rest day or night ...

God is very clear that Hell is a terrible place.

Suppose the talk about fire and brimstone is not literal, that it is just a symbol for something else. What must that something else be, that God would use such a horrifying symbol to explain it? If the fire is "just" an analogy, then the reality must still be equally terrible.

This theory explains nothing.

8.4. Is suffering in Hell eternal?

The traditional Christian view is that the unsaved suffer in Hell forever.

An opposing view is that God destroys the souls of the unsaved after death. That is, rather than suffering for eternity, the unsaved cease to exist. This is called "Annihilationism". It is taught by Jehovah's Witnesses, Seventh Day Adventists, Christian Scientists, and others.

(Technically, Seventh Day Adventists teach "soul sleep", by which they mean that the unsaved are unconscious for eternity. In practice this seems little different from Annihilationism.)

The Annihilationist argument basically goes like this:

Matthew 19:16 Now behold, one came and said to Him, "Good Teacher, what good thing shall I do that I may have eternal life?"

If one must meet certain conditions to have eternal life, than that must mean that people who don't meet those conditions don't have eternal life.

John 3:16 For God so loved the world that He gave His only begotten Son, that whoever believes in Him should not perish but have everlasting life.

Philippians 3:18-19 For many walk, of whom I have told you often, and now tell you even weeping, that they are the enemies of the cross of Christ: whose end is destruction, whose god is their belly, and whose glory is in their shame—who set their mind on earthly things.

These verses and others like them don't contrast eternity in Paradise with eternity in Hell, but rather eternal life with "perishing" or "destruction".

The main argument is probably philosophical more than scriptural. To the Annihilationists, for God to punish people with eternal torment would make him cruel and unjust. It makes God the commandant of a concentration camp. In a person's lifetime he can only commit a finite amount of sin, and a finite amount of sin does not deserve an infinite punishment.

This sort of logical, philosophical reasoning is fine grounds to form a theory, but it is not proof. Ultimately the only way we can know about Heaven and Hell – before we die and see the truth for ourselves, anyway – is from scripture.

Annihilationists quote verses saying that the unsaved will be "destroyed", which they interpret as "cease to exist".

But many Bible verses very clearly say that they will spend eternity in Hell.

Matthew 25:41,46 Then He will also say to those on the left hand, "Depart from Me, you cursed, into the everlasting fire prepared for the devil and his angels." ... And these will go away into everlasting punishment, but the righteous into eternal life."

The unsaved go to "everlasting punishment", not to

annihilation.

Note the parallel construction: one group to "everlasting punishment" but the other to "eternal life". If you read the phrase "eternal life" by itself, you might reasonably think that the opposite of "eternal life" is "finite life", that is, that "eternal life" means living forever and the opposite is then to live for a finite amount of time. But here it is clear that the opposite of eternal life is not annihilation but everlasting punishment. Apparently God's idea of "life" is not simply "existence", but a certain kind of existence.

Annihilationists reply that ceasing to exist is final, so this is "everlasting punishment".

> John 5:28-29 Do not marvel at this; for the hour is coming in which all who are in the graves will hear His voice and come forth — those who have done good, to the resurrection of life, and those who have done evil, to the resurrection of condemnation.

Both the saved and the unsaved will be resurrected. The difference is not that the saved are resurrected and the unsaved are not, but where they go after this resurrection. And note again that the opposite of "life" is not "annihilation" but "condemnation".

We could quote many other verses that describe eternal punishment in Hell.

So what are we to make of the verses that talk about the unsaved being destroyed? Doesn't this mean that the souls of the unsaved cease to exist? Not necessarily.

The Greek word for "destruction" in Philippians 3:19 is "apoleia". This is the same word used in Revelation to describe what happens to the Beast:

> Revelation 17:8 The beast that you saw was, and is not, and will ascend out of the bottomless pit and go to perdition [apoleia].

But if we read ahead a few chapters we find this description of what happens to the Beast:

> Revelation 20:10 The devil, who deceived them, was cast into the lake of fire and brimstone where the beast and the false prophet are. And they will be tormented day and night forever and ever.

So Revelation 17 says that the Beast will go to "apoleia" – he will be destroyed. But Revelation 20, written by the same person at the same time, says the Beast (along with the Devil and the False Prophet) will be tormented forever in the Lake of Fire. So "destruction" -- "apoleia" -- does not mean that he will cease to exist, but that he will be completely defeated. We often use English words like "destruction" this way, too. When we say, "The football team destroyed its opposition", we don't mean that the losing team was disbanded or that all the team members were killed and their bodies burned, but simply that they suffered a serious defeat. Similarly when we say things like, "The car was destroyed in the accident," we normally don't mean that no trace of the car exists any more. We mean that it was very badly damaged.

Annihilationists generally concede that Satan is punished forever and that therefore the Lake of Fire exists forever. They say that when Satan is thrown in the Lake of Fire, he suffers forever, but when humans are thrown in the Lake of Fire, they are annihilated.

So regardless of the philosophical arguments, scripture pretty clearly teaches that the unsaved suffer for eternity. You may think this is unfair or unjust or you don't like the idea, but that's not evidence that it's false. I don't like the idea that I could get hurt if I fall down the stairs, but that's not evidence against the theory of gravity.

If we must conclude that the unsaved suffer for eternity, does it therefore follow that God is unjust? No.

What of the claim that a finite amount of sin does not deserve an infinite punishment? That assumes that the sin is finite. Some have argued that even one sin is infinitely evil and deserves an infinite punishment. I'd say that this argument is based on the assumption that a person stops sinning when he dies. But this is not necessarily so. We don't know much about what life in Hell is like. We'll discuss the nature of the suffering in Hell in section 8.5, which may or may not be relevant here. People are in Hell because they rejected God and his laws. Maybe they continue to do so in Hell. Do people in Hell have possessions? They might steal from each other. They might fight. They could certainly hate and blaspheme. They could be sent to Hell for sins committed on Earth, but they remain in Hell because of sins committed in Hell.

8.5. Is Hell punishment or "just" separation from God?

There are two views on the nature of the suffering in Hell. One is that Hell is a place where God actively and continuously punishes the unsaved. The other is that it is a place of separation from God, and the suffering is caused by the absence of God's presence.

There is some evidence in scripture to support either position.

Luke 12:47-48 And that servant who knew his master's will, and did not prepare himself or do according to his will, shall be beaten with many stripes. But he who did not know, yet committed things deserving of stripes, shall be beaten with few.

This is from a parable so we have to be careful about taking it literally. But it is talking about punishment for sin. If someone is being beaten, that implies that someone is doing the beating, which would indicate active punishment.

2 Thessalonians 1:6-8 Since it is a righteous thing with God to repay with tribulation those who trouble you, and to give you who are troubled rest with us when the Lord Jesus is revealed from heaven with His mighty angels, in flaming fire taking vengeance on those who do not know God, and on those who do not obey the gospel of our Lord Jesus Christ.

Angels will carry out the punishment of the wicked.

Rev 14:9-11 He shall be tormented with fire and brimstone in the presence of the holy angels and in the presence of the Lamb.

Punishment will be carried out in the presence of the angels.

Other verses indicate that Hell is separation from God.

Matthew 25:10-12 ... the bridegroom came, and those who were ready went in with him to the wedding; and the door was shut. Afterward the other virgins came also, saying, 'Lord, Lord, open to us!' But he answered and said, 'Assuredly, I say to you, I do not know you.'

If you read the whole context, this is a story Jesus tells to make the point that people should be prepared for his return. Those who are prepared will go into "the wedding", they will be with Jesus. Those who are not prepared will be left outside, out of his presence.

This is a parable and not a literal description, but still, the unprepared are locked out of Christ's presence, not beaten or tortured.

Matthew 25:30 And cast the unprofitable servant into the outer darkness. There will be weeping and gnashing of teeth.

The unsaved are thrown into the "outer darkness". They are locked out of Christ's presence.

Even the verses that might at first make us think that God is personally and actively punishing the unsaved are consistent with the idea of separation from God.

Luke 12 doesn't say who is doing the beating, just that sinners will suffer.

2 Thessalonians sounds like it is describing active punishment, but read just a couple of verses further down:

2 Thessalonians 1:9 These shall be punished with everlasting destruction from the presence of the Lord and from the glory of His power,

God punishes those who reject him ... but the punishment is "destruction from the presence of the Lord".

Revelation says that the unsaved will be punished "in the presence of" angels", but it doesn't say that the punishment is done "by" angels.

The Catechism of the Catholic Church is consistent with the idea of separation:

1035 The teaching of the Church affirms the existence of hell and its eternity. Immediately after death the souls of those who die in a state of mortal sin descend into hell, where they suffer the punishments of hell, "eternal fire". The chief punishment of hell is eternal separation from God, in whom alone man can possess the life and happiness for which he was created and for which he longs. (http://www.usccb.org/beliefs-and-teachings/what-we-believe/catechism/catechism-of-the-catholic-church/epub/index.cfm)

The unsaved want nothing to do with God. They don't want to live under his laws. They just want him to get out of their way. Perhaps Hell is just God giving the unsaved exactly what they want: freedom from his presence and his rules.

What would such a place be like? Of course atheists routinely talk about how wonderful the world would be if only everyone would give up their crazy superstitions. They blame many of the world's problems on religion, especially Christianity.

But look at societies where the atheists' dream of Christianity being rejected was actually achieved. The first atheist society in history that I know of was revolutionary France of 1789 to 1799. They started out with high hopes and fine words, like publishing the "Declaration of the Rights of Man and the Citizen", which promised all sorts of civil rights. But once the atheists actually came to power, they declared the Declaration "suspended" and implemented what they themselves called "the Terror". Anyone who opposed the government or even complained about bad conditions, like the food shortages that they caused, was subject to arrest and execution. They promised religious freedom but tortured and killed Christians, especially the clergy. In the end they turned on each other, and many of the leaders died on the same guillotine they had used to kill others.

The other major atheist societies in history are Stalin's Soviet Union, Mao's China, Pol Pot's Cambodia, and modern North Korea. The Soviet Union started with fine ideals about rescuing the common people from rich oppressors and freeing all human beings to achieve their full potential. Similar things could be said about the others. Most readers are probably familiar with how these social experiments turned out. All engaged in mass murder and brutal persecution of all who disagreed with them, or who were suspected of disagreeing with them, or who they thought might disagree with them someday. Stalin had at least 22 million people killed. Mao caused the deaths of 50 million people.

Pol Pot only killed 2 million people. In absolute numbers he was an amateur compared to Mao and Stalin. But Pol Pot only had a population of 8 million to start with and was only in power for 4 years. So in that short time he killed 25% of the population of his own country.

Compare this to horrors of religious extremism that atheists like to point to. Over the course of 400 years the Spanish Inquisition killed 4000 people, about half of them Jews and half Protestants. As a Protestant, I don't accept responsibility for the actions of people whose stated goal was to destroy Protestantism. I doubt that most of the people involved with the Inquisition could even fairly be described as extremist Catholics: mostly they were people using the Catholic Church to advance their own political power. But even if we accept the idea that the Inquisition was Christianity run amok, if Christians are responsible for the Inquisition, then atheists must accept responsibility for Mao and Stalin. Yes, the Inquisition was cruel, and those 4000 deaths are 4000 terrible tragedies. But if a *day* went by when Stalin's minions didn't kill 4000 people, he would have been disappointed. He probably would have had the executioners killed for failing to carry out their duties zealously enough.

The Salem witch trials don't even register compared to Mao and Stalin: a total of 19 killed. And by the way, the leading preachers of the time opposed the witch trials and published books and pamphlets condemning the trials.

Let me make clear that I am not saying that all atheists are evil, violent people. Quite the contrary, most atheists that I have met are reasonably decent fellows. But most atheists that I have met live in a society where Christian ethics are the accepted norm. What happens when a society rejects that norm? The empirical evidence is that a society that rejects God and his laws starts with high ideals about freedom and human potential, but ends with tyranny, repression, and mass murder.

(By the way, if an atheist reads this and is outraged at my characterization of the consequences of atheism, let's bear in mind that what I've said here is milder than what atheists often say about Christianity. And, I think, better grounded in historical reality.)

Note this interesting description of God's judgment in Romans:

Romans 1:18,24-26a,28-32 For the wrath of God is revealed from heaven against all ungodliness and unrighteousness of men, who suppress the truth in unrighteousness, ... Therefore God also gave them up to uncleanness, in the lusts of their hearts, to dishonor their bodies among themselves, who exchanged the truth of God for the lie, and worshiped and served the creature rather than the Creator, who is blessed forever. Amen. For this reason God gave them up to vile passions. ... And even as they did not like to retain God in their knowledge, God gave them over to a debased mind, to do those things which are not fitting; being filled with all unrighteousness, sexual immorality, wickedness, covetousness, maliciousness; full of envy, murder, strife, deceit, evil-mindedness; they are whisperers, backbiters, haters of God, violent, proud, boasters, inventors of evil things, disobedient to parents, undiscerning, untrustworthy, unloving, unforgiving, unmerciful; who, knowing the righteous judgment of God, that those who practice such things are deserving of death, not only do the same but also approve of those who practice them.

How does it say God revealed his wrath in this case? By letting people do exactly what they want, and then suffer the natural consequences.

So here is my theory. Admittedly this is highly speculative.

The unsaved want nothing to do with God. They may be outright atheists who deny that he even exists. Others concede that he exists but don't acknowledge his authority. In either case, they don't want to follow God's rules.

So suppose God gives them what they want. He puts them in some place where he withdraws his presence. They can then do whatever they please.

What would happen? Probably just what happens when people try to separate themselves from God here on this Earth, but more so. They would indulge in cheap sex, drug and alcohol abuse, exploitation, tyranny, and violence. Lots of violence. Presumably they can't murder each other because they are all immortal souls. Maybe other sins are not possible in Hell. If so, they'll find analogous things.

In this scenario, it would not be "necessary" for God to personally punish these people. They would punish themselves and each other. Forever.

What about Hell being a place of fire? Two possibilities.

The traditional view is that the place God sends these people is filled with fire that he has put there to punish them.

Another possibility is that the people there create the fires themselves. Perhaps people in Hell are forever trying to build things – homes, factories, etc – and then others burn them down. They build weapons to attack each other. And so on. And so the place is a constant battlefield, filled with guns and bombs (or some equivalent of guns and bombs) and fire. They can't kill each other, because they are already dead. But they can still hurt each other and destroy things.

Recall that Jesus used the word "Gehenna" to refer to Hell. (Section 6.4.) The fires in Gehenna were not put there by God. They were started by people, who used the fires to burn their own children to death.

8.6.   Does the Devil rule Hell?

One element of the popular view of Eternity is that God rules Heaven and the Devil rules Hell.

Nowhere does the Bible say that the Devil rules Hell. Rather the opposite.

> Revelation 20:10 The devil, who deceived them, was cast into the lake of fire and brimstone where the beast and the false prophet are. And they will be tormented day and night forever and ever.

The Devil does not rule in Hell. He is a prisoner there.

In section 6.6 we talked about Abaddon, an angel who rules the Abyss. If the Abyss is Hell, if these are two names for the same place, then the ruler of Hell is Abaddon. If they are not the same place, then the Bible gives no clue who rules Hell.

If, as I theorize in section 8.5, Hell is a place where God gives people and demons free reign to do as they wish, it is possible that the Devil manages to make himself powerful there in a political or military sense. If he does rule, he is ruling like the leader of a gang in a prison, not as the warden.

8.7.   Why does God send people to Hell?

Why does God send anyone to Hell? If God is truly loving, why doesn't he just admit everyone to Paradise?

But what if God did admit everyone to Paradise? What would happen then?

Would everyone be required to obey God's laws? If not, then Paradise would be just as filled with crime and violence and drug abuse and hate and sexual depravity and so on as the Earth is. It wouldn't be Paradise.

If God forced everyone in Paradise to obey his laws, then he'd be taking away their freedom. The classic Christian response to the question of, "Why is there evil in the world?" has always been, "Because God gave people free will." If God admitted everyone to Paradise and then prevented them from sinning, we would all have to be mindless robots. Or perhaps people would know that they don't want to do the things that God is forcing them to do, but they are powerless to control their own bodies. This wouldn't be Paradise, but its own kind of Hell. In any case, if God was going to do that in Paradise, why doesn't he do that on Earth, and eliminate all the suffering that sin causes?

People go to Hell because they want to be in Hell. Not that they want the suffering of Hell, but they want the separation from God. They do not want to obey God's laws. People on Earth who reject God are often convinced that they can create paradise without God, indeed that the idea of God interferes with creating paradise. Just listen to secular humanists. Well, some do want the suffering of Hell. For some, a paradise of people living together in peace and harmony is the last thing they want. There are tyrants and criminals who like nothing better than causing as much suffering and destruction as they can. Neither group wants to be in God's Paradise. And God respects that choice.

8.8.   Is there a second chance?

One theory is that a person can be saved at any moment up until death, and then his chance has passed. By this theory, Hell is a place of eternal punishment and suffering.

Another theory is that it is possible to be saved after death. This has been called PME: Post Mortem Evangelism. By this theory, Hell is God's last way to finally get a person's attention. For example, Mormons teach that people who have never heard the Gospel or who rejected it in life will go to "spirit prison" where they have another chance.

Advocates of PME quote verses such as:

John 5:25 Most assuredly, I say to you, the hour is coming, and now is, when the dead will hear the voice of the Son of God; and those who hear will live.

This seems to say that Jesus will preach to the dead, and that they will have an opportunity to respond.

But going ahead just a few verses undercuts this interpretation.

John 5:28b-29 For the hour is coming in which all who are in the graves will hear His voice and come forth — those who have done good, to the resurrection of life, and those who have done evil, to the resurrection of condemnation.

Apparently the idea is that, yes, Jesus will preach to the dead and those who listen will enjoy eternal life. But who will listen and who will not appears to depend on what they did in life. This verse casts significant doubt on the idea that they have a second chance after death.

Another proof text for PME:

1 Corinthians 15:19 If in this life only we have hope in Christ, we are of all men the most pitiable.

But in context, Paul isn't saying that the unsaved have another hope after this life, but rather that the saved have hopes beyond the current life. If someone is being persecuted for being a Christian, then if this life is all there is, why be a Christian if it just causes you trouble? The reason is that we believe that this life is *not* all there is, and that any suffering in this life is more than made up for in Eternity.

1 Peter 4:6a For this reason the gospel was preached also to those who are dead.

Why would God preach the Gospel to the dead, except to give them a chance to repent?

But the second half of the verse gives a reason:

1 Peter 4:6b … that they might be judged according to men in the flesh, but live according to God in the spirit.

The verse most commonly quoted to refute PME is:

Hebrew 9:27-28a And as it is appointed for men to die once, but after this the judgment, so Christ was offered once to bear the sins of many.

Christ died once, we each die once, and we each face judgment once.

Luke 16:19-26 There was a certain rich man who was clothed in purple and fine linen and fared sumptuously every day. But there was a certain beggar named Lazarus, full of sores, who was laid at his gate, desiring to be fed with the crumbs which fell from the rich man's table. Moreover the dogs came and licked his sores. So it was that the beggar died, and was carried by the angels to Abraham's bosom. The rich man also died and was buried. And being in torments in Hades, he lifted up his eyes and saw Abraham afar off, and Lazarus in his bosom. Then he cried and said, 'Father Abraham, have mercy on me, and send Lazarus that he may dip the tip of his finger in water and cool my tongue; for I am tormented in this flame.' But Abraham said, 'Son, remember that in your lifetime you received your good things, and likewise Lazarus evil things; but now he is comforted and you are tormented. And besides all this, between us and you there is a great gulf fixed, so that those who want to pass from here to you cannot, nor can those from there pass to us.'

When the rich man is in Hades and has an opportunity to make a request of Abraham, he does not ask to be released from Hades. He just asks for some water. If there is a second chance after death, wouldn't he have declared that he has now realized his mistake and wants to be saved, rather than just asking for some relief from the horrors of Hades? Or why didn't Abraham say, "I can give you better than a drop of water: If you repent now, you can be released from Hades." Instead he says rather the opposite. He says that there is a great gulf that prevents anyone passing from the place of torment to the place of happiness. The rich man is stuck in Hades.

Matthew 25:1-4 Then the kingdom of heaven shall be likened to ten virgins who took their lamps and went out to meet the bridegroom. Now five of them were wise, and five were foolish. Those who were foolish took their lamps and took no oil with them, but the wise took oil in their vessels with their lamps.

If you are not familiar with this parable, feel free to look it up and read the whole story. The point of the story is that some of the women were prepared for the arrival of the bridegroom, and so were able to enter and enjoy the wedding, while others were not prepared, and so were locked out of the wedding. Jesus explained that this was a parable about his second coming: some people would be prepared, and others not.

The story only makes sense if there is no second chance. If there was a second chance, it wouldn't end with the women who were unprepared being locked out in the darkness. It would have ended with them getting more oil for their lamps, coming back, and attending the wedding. The whole point of the story is that these women did *not* get a second chance. They missed their one chance.

Indeed, I wonder: If people in Hell were given a second chance, if God said to them, I will admit you to Paradise, all you have to do is accept my offer of salvation and agree to abide by my rules, how many would say, "Kowtow to you? Follow your rules? No way. Hell is terrible, but there's no way I'm putting up with that."

It seems there is no "second chance". Once a person dies, he faces judgment, and that's it. It would be pleasant to believe that people could escape from Hell and that eventually everyone will be saved and Hell will be empty. But there's no Biblical reason to believe such a thing. It's just a pleasant fantasy.

8.9. Degrees of reward and punishment

Equality Theory: In Paradise, everyone is equal and enjoys the same rewards. Likewise, in Hell everyone is equal and suffers the same punishment.

Justice Theory: There are levels of rewards in Paradise and levels of punishment in Hell. People who have been the most faithful and who have done extraordinary good works deserve and receive special rewards. People who have been the most evil deserve and receive special punishments.

Both theories have logical, philosophical sense behind them.

Proponents of the equality theory point out that the whole foundation of Christianity is that you are not saved because of your good works, but entirely by grace.

Ephesians 2:8-9 For by grace you have been saved through faith, and that not of yourselves; it is the gift of God, not of works, lest anyone should boast.

You cannot earn anything in God's sight, because you are a sinner.

Romans 3:23 For all have sinned and fall short of the glory of God.

Some Bible verses can be taken to mean that God views all sin equally. Like:

James 2:10-12 For whoever shall keep the whole law, and yet stumble in one point, he is guilty of all. For He who said, "Do not commit adultery," also said, "Do not murder." Now if you do not commit adultery, but you do murder, you have become a transgressor of the law.

The point in context is that if you have broken one of God's commandments, it is worthless to argue that you never broke some other commandment. You are still guilty of sin. (And of course we all have broken at least some of God's commandments.)

Even the most seemingly trivial of sins are deserving of Hell.

Matthew 5:21 "You have heard that it was said to those of old, 'You shall not murder, and whoever murders will be in danger of the judgment.' But I say to you that whoever is angry with his brother without a cause shall be in danger of the judgment. And whoever says to his brother, 'Raca!' shall be in danger of the council. But whoever says, 'You fool!' shall be in danger of hell fire.

("Raca" was the equivalent of a harsh swear word in Jesus time.)

I think most people concede that it is justice for a murderer to go to Hell. Many see blasphemy as a reason why God would send people to Hell. But here Jesus says that just being unfairly angry with your brother or calling someone a fool are bad enough sins to send someone to Hell.

Perhaps the most explicit discussion of this point is the parable of the workers in the vineyard. It's an important story, and it's difficult to summarize, so let me quote it in full:

Matthew 20:1-15 For the kingdom of heaven is like a landowner who went out early in the morning to hire laborers for his vineyard. Now when he had agreed with the laborers for a denarius a day, he sent them into his vineyard. And he went out about the third hour [9:00 am] and saw others standing idle in the marketplace, and said to them, 'You also go into the vineyard, and whatever is right I will give you.' So they went. Again he went out about the sixth [noon] and the ninth hour [3:00 pm], and did likewise. And about the eleventh hour [5:00 pm] he went out and found others standing idle, and said to them, 'Why have you been standing here idle all day?' They said to him, 'Because no one hired us.' He said to them, 'You also go into the vineyard, and whatever is right you will receive.'

"So when evening had come, the owner of the vineyard said to his steward, 'Call the laborers and give them their wages, beginning with the last to the first.' And when those came who were hired about the eleventh hour, they each received a denarius. But when the first came, they supposed that they would receive more; and they likewise received each a denarius. And when they had received it, they complained against the landowner, saying, 'These last men have worked only one hour, and you made them equal to us who have borne the burden and the heat of the day.' But he answered one of them and said, 'Friend, I am doing you no wrong. Did you not agree with me for a denarius? Take what is yours and go your way. I wish to give to this last man the same as to you. Is it not lawful for me to do what I wish with my own things? Or is your eye evil because I am good?'

Christianity says that salvation is by grace alone. If you spend your entire life as a missionary in some third world country, working to help the poor and the oppressed at great personal sacrifice, after you die you spend eternity in Paradise. If you spend your entire life as a serial killer who tortures and kills small children because you think it's funny to hear them beg, and then on your death bed you repent and accept Christ, after you die you spend eternity in Paradise. Non-Christians often ask, "How can this be fair? Shouldn't the person who lives a good life and sacrifices for others get a greater reward?"

Jesus answered that question 2000 years ago.

The people in the story who worked 12 hours in the hot sun received a denarius. At that time one denarius was the conventional pay for one day of manual labor. The amount they were promised was a fair amount, or at least the amount anyone would have expected to get. It wasn't generous, but no one would say they were being cheated. It was the same amount they would have been paid if they'd worked for someone else.

But then the people who only worked half a day, or even for just one hour, are also paid a denarius. Getting a full day's pay for just one hour of work certainly is generous, far more than they could claim to have deserved. And so the people who worked all day complain: How come they got the same amount for one hour that we got for a whole day? And note Jesus's reply: You agreed that this was a fair amount. How have you been cheated? Yes, I gave someone else more than he deserved. But I did not give you any less than you deserved.

Do you see the analogy? A person who worked and served for God and for his fellow humans for his whole life was told at the start what the reward was: eternity in Paradise. Apparently he considered this a fair deal, because he accepted it. And you might say that it is a fair deal: he worked hard and sacrificed a lot, and in return he was given a big reward.

A person who did nothing for God or for other people for his whole life, who perhaps even did all he could to hurt other people, but on his death bed turns to Christ, also receives eternity in Paradise. Does he deserve that? Clearly, obviously not. What he deserves is to go to Hell. But God is merciful and generous, and gives him something far better than he deserves.

But he's not cheating the faithful worker by doing this. The faithful worker is not getting less than he deserves.

I would add that we should be glad that God is *not* fair. Even the person who serves his whole life still commits many sins. He does not live up to God's standard of perfect holiness. If God was fair, we would all go to Hell. But lucky for us, God is not fair. He is generous.

All that said, there are Bible verses that indicate that there are levels of reward in Paradise.

> Matthew 19:28-30 So Jesus said to them, "Assuredly I say to you, that in the regeneration, when the Son of Man sits on the throne of His glory, you who have followed Me will also sit on twelve thrones, judging the twelve tribes of Israel. And everyone who has left houses or brothers or sisters or father or mother or wife or children or lands, for My name's sake, shall receive a hundredfold, and inherit eternal life. But many who are first will be last, and the last first.

In Eternity, the saved who gave up family or wealth for Christ will be rewarded in proportion to what they gave up. Apparently those who gave up a lot for God will get more than those who only gave up a little.

> Matthew 16:27 For the Son of Man will come in the glory of His Father with His angels, and then He will reward each according to his works.

> Revelation 22:12 And behold, I am coming quickly, and My reward is with Me, to give to every one according to his work.

Again, reward "according to his works".

> Matthew 10:14-15 And whoever will not receive you nor hear your words, when you depart from that house or city, shake off the dust from your feet. Assuredly, I say to you, it will be more tolerable for the land of Sodom and Gomorrah in the day of judgment than for that city!

There are levels of punishment in Hell. Here and elsewhere,

Jesus says that people who saw great miracles performed and still rejected God will be judged more severely than those who did not have an opportunity to see miracles.

How can we reconcile verses that seem to say there is no difference with verses that say there is a difference?

I think the connection is this:

> 1 Corinthians 3:11-15 For no other foundation can anyone lay than that which is laid, which is Jesus Christ. Now if anyone builds on this foundation with gold, silver, precious stones, wood, hay, straw, each one's work will become clear; for the Day will declare it, because it will be revealed by fire; and the fire will test each one's work, of what sort it is. If anyone's work which he has built on it endures, he will receive a reward. If anyone's work is burned, he will suffer loss; but he himself will be saved, yet so as through fire.

The most important thing is whether or not you are saved. And salvation does not depend on works. Even if a person does nothing for God, he does not lose his salvation.

But what a saved person does for God can earn him rewards.

Everyone who is saved gets the "minimum", eternal life with Christ. And what a minimum! But after that, on top of that, there are additional rewards for those who have done particularly good deeds.

8.10. Do the saved see Hell?

I often hear Christians say that they think that people in Paradise will not be able to see Hell, and will not remember unsaved friends and relatives. Otherwise, they say, how could Paradise be a place of joy and happiness? Everyone would be too upset seeing the suffering in Hell and knowing that people they cared about were among those suffering.

This is an interesting idea, and a plausible idea, but it is not found in the Bible. It is something people invented for philosophical reasons. But this theory faces the fundamental problem that the only "evidence" for it is the subjective emotional response of the people who propose it. There is no real reply to the obvious objection, "Who says?"

It *might* be true.

Or maybe people can enjoy Paradise despite knowledge of the

existence of Hell. You know that there is all sorts of pain and suffering in the world: the homeless, the starving, abandoned orphans, victims of persecution. Does this knowledge prevent you from enjoying your life? Probably not. And this is unjustified suffering. Okay, maybe we ignore these things because of our lack of compassion. If we were perfect human beings, it would disturb us more.

Does the fact that there are prisons in the world prevent you from enjoying your life? What if you knew that everyone in the prison deserved to be there and was getting exactly the punishment he deserved? If we were perfect human beings, would we not appreciate justice?

Many of us have friends or family members who have ruined their lives through willful bad choices. You may know people who have committed crimes and gotten caught, abused drugs or alcohol and become addicts, etc. Or maybe not that dramatic, but they're lazy and irresponsible and so can't get a decent job, or they continually get romantically involved with people who are clearly bad news and go from one heartbreak to another, etc. If so, do you spend your life constantly worrying and crying about how bad this person's life is? Maybe I'm being harsh, but I know people like that, and I don't. You try to help, but at some point you say, You've made your decisions, you've rejected all the good advice you've ever been given by me and everyone else who cares about you, I'm sorry but there's no more I can do for you. And you move on.

Maybe that's how people in Paradise will think about people in Hell: You had the choice, and you choose wrong. There's nothing more I can do for you.

8.11. Marriage & Sex

Is their marriage in Paradise? Will you still be married to your husband or wife when you get there?

Jesus was specifically asked this question. Read Matthew 22:23-33. The Sadducees presented Jesus with this puzzle: A woman married, and then her husband died. Of course a widow is allowed to remarry, and so she did. And then the second husband died and she remarried again, etc, for a total of seven husbands. So, they asked Jesus, who will she be married to in Eternity? Will she have seven husbands?

Jesus replies: "For in the resurrection they neither marry nor are given in marriage, but are like angels of God in heaven."

The Sadducees did not believe in eternal life, so they thought they had Jesus caught in a stumper. Either he had to say that Old Testament laws that say you can remarry when your spouse dies are wrong, and thus that God made a mistake when he gave those laws; or he had to say that a woman could have more than one husband in Paradise, which would create the paradox that people in Paradise can break the laws God gave us here on Earth; or he would have to "admit" that there cannot be any such thing as eternal life. But Jesus surprised them with an entirely different sort of answer: there is no marriage in Paradise.

(Of course by the same reasoning a man who divorced and remarried would have multiple wives. And one can imagine all sorts of complex scenarios. What if Alice and Bob marry, then Alice dies and Bob marries Cathy, then Bob dies and Cathy marries David. In Eternity is Bob married to both Alice and Cathy, while simultaneously Cathy is married to both Bob and David? Or is there one big group marriage of Alice, Bob, Cathy, and David?)

Two side notes on this story before we get back to the question at hand:

One: The Sadducees thought they had found a contradiction in orthodox teaching. But Jesus explained that the solution was not that either of the seemingly contradictory statements was false, but that the correct answer was in an entirely different direction, a direction they had not even considered. This is something to keep in mind when we run into statements in the Bible that appear to contradict each other or what we think we know from science or history or other sources. Maybe the simple answer is that we would see that both are true, if only we were smart or creative enough.

Two: Jesus goes on to prove that there is eternal life. And here is how he proves it: "Have you not read what was spoken to you by God, saying, 'I am the God of Abraham, the God of Isaac, and the God of Jacob'? God is not the God of the dead, but of the living." Do you get it? He quotes an Old Testament verse where God says, "I am the God of Abraham", etc. And his whole point is: At the time that God says this, Abraham was dead. So if there is no eternal life, God would have said, "I *was* the God of Abraham", because Abraham would no longer exist. But God didn't say that. He said, "I *am* the God of Abraham." Thus Abraham must still exist. Jesus entire argument rested, not just on one word from Scripture, but on the tense of the verb, the fact that it was in what in English we call present tense rather than past tense. (Hebrew verb tenses are not the same as English, but the same principle applies.)

Often today when people don't want to believe the plain language of the Bible, they brush it off by taking liberties with the language. Jesus not only took the Old Testament literally, but he took it literally right down to the verb tenses.

But getting back to the point ...

Some people who say they believe the Bible nevertheless insist that, despite these verses, there is marriage in Eternity. Mormons and Swedenborgians believe in "eternal marriage", that is, that marriage is not "til death do us part", but rather is for all eternity. Technically, Mormons believe that marriages performed in a Mormon temple by someone with the proper "sealing authority" – what they call "celestial marriages" -- are eternal, and that other marriages only last until death.

They cite Matthew 16. Jesus says to Peter:

Matthew 16:19 Whatever you bind on earth will be bound in heaven, and whatever you loose on earth will be loosed in heaven.

Thus, they say, a marriage bound on Earth by a duly authorized priest is equally binding in Heaven.

They also quote their own sacred book, *Doctrine & Covenants,* but of course non-Mormons do not consider that authoritative.

Other advocates of the idea of eternal marriage say:

(a) What Jesus meant was that there will be no *new* marriages made in Eternity, but that marriages made in this life will continue.

(b) Jesus was talking about corrupted marriages, that is, marriages made for the wrong reasons or where the couple did not live up to God's principles for marriage. But "spiritual marriages" will last for eternity.

(c) They quote:

Matthew 19:4-6 And He answered and said to them, "Have you not read that He who made them at the beginning 'made them male and female,' and said, 'For this reason a man shall leave his father and mother and be joined to his wife, and the two shall become one flesh'? So then, they are no longer two but one flesh. Therefore what God has joined together, let not man separate."

But none of these arguments really hold up in light of Jesus's statements.

Jesus didn't say that some marriages are eternal and some end at death. He said that in eternity people do not marry, period. If he had meant that some marriages continue into eternity, his argument would have fallen apart. Has there ever been a woman whose husband died and who then remarried, and for whom both marriages "qualified" as eternal marriages? If so, then he has not answered the original question. To say it doesn't happen all the time doesn't resolve the question of when it does happen.

Mormons get around this by saying that only a "celestial marriage" is eternal, and other marriages are not. Presumably they do not declare more than one marriage per person to be eternal. So if Alice marries Bob in a celestial marriage, and then Bob dies and she marries Charles in an ordinary marriage, then when Alice dies, in Eternity she is married to Bob again, and her marriage to Charles is over. Interesting idea, but not what Jesus said. If this was the solution to the problem of multiple husbands that the Sadducees brought up, Jesus would not have said that it is a non-issue because people in Eternity do not marry. He would have said that the problem is resolved because at most one marriage per person is eternal and the others end at death. Jesus answer was nothing at all like the Mormon answer.

When Jesus made the statement about "binding in heaven", he was not talking about marriage. It's possible that his intent was that this principle includes marriage, but he doesn't say whether it does or doesn't. Even if we assume it does, it could just as well be taken to mean that when the Church declares a couple married, God in Heaven recognizes this as binding just as it is recognized on Earth, without any implication that therefore it continues beyond death.

Theorizing that Jesus meant that there are no new marriages in Heaven but that marriages made on Earth continue destroys the whole point of his argument. The case the Sadducees brought to Jesus was about a woman who had seven marriages *on Earth*. If Jesus had meant that she could not marry yet an eighth man in Heaven after she died, that would have done nothing to explain what would happen with the first seven men.

Finally, the relevance of "what God has joined let man not separate" is not at all clear. I suppose you could say that if we believe that death ends a marriage, then if someone murders a woman's husband, this would end the marriage, and then a man is separating what God has joined together, and so this contradicts Jesus's statement. Of course it wouldn't have to be something as dramatic as murder: it could be causing an accident or causing your own death by smoking too much or whatever. But many deaths are not caused by men. Plenty of people die of old age, disease, and natural disasters. No "man" is ending the marriage in this case, it is forces of nature. If we understood Jesus to be saying that an act of man that causes death does not end a marriage, we would still be left with all the cases where people died in ways not caused by man. Again, this does not answer the Sadducees question. It's more logical to understand Jesus's words here the way they have traditionally been interpreted: as barring divorce, not saying that murder does not end a marriage.

So the only reasonable way to understand Jesus's words is: There is no marriage in Eternity. Marriage is "til death do us part".

Does this mean there is no sex in Paradise? The Bible plainly teaches that sex is supposed to be limited to married couples. So if there is no marriage, then there can be no sex.

I'd say, maybe, but not necessarily. Clearly life in Paradise is different in many ways from life on Earth. There is no death. There is no sin. We are in fellowship with God. I have a hard time imagining that God would say that in Paradise promiscuity is now legal, but perhaps he has some other relationship to regulate sex.

Many commentators say that there is no need for sex in Paradise because plenty of people have been born here on Earth, so there are enough souls to populate Paradise. But as we have already discussed, New Jerusalem is huge. Even if every human who has ever been born would live there – which is, of course, not true, only a minority are saved – it would still be a very sparsely-populated place. And the universe is incredibly huge. Astronomers estimate that there are 200 billion to 400 billion stars in our galaxy alone. We have little idea how many stars have planets, but even if it's only a small percentage, there could easily be hundreds of millions of planets. And our galaxy is only one of many. There are far too many galaxies to count, but it's estimated that several hundred billion can be seen with our telescopes. There are at least several *trillion* stars for every human being who has ever lived. Why would God create such a huge universe, if he didn't intend for people to fill it? And we have nowhere near enough people in the world today to even begin to fill a tiny portion of it. We have yet to truly fill our one little planet.

That said, I've heard Christians fret that they want to be sure to get married and have sex before they die because they're afraid that there won't be any sex in Paradise and they don't want to miss out. I wouldn't worry that we are going to miss it. If God takes something away, it will surely be because he replaces it with something better. When we're in Paradise, if there is no sex, I'm sure we'll be too busy doing other fun and exciting things that God has for us to be worried about the absence of sex. I suspect there are pleasures that we enjoy here on Earth that we will look back on in Eternity as childish amusements. Like, now that I am an adult, I no longer draw in coloring books. I do not cry and moan because I am "not allowed" to draw in coloring books now that I am an adult. Rather, I have no desire to do this anymore because I have moved on to more adult pleasures, and the idea of drawing in a coloring book just seems boring.

8.12. Resurrection body

What will our bodies be like after the resurrection? The Bible does not give a very clear description, but it does give some clues.

Often we think that in Eternity we will not have bodies; that our souls or spirits will float freely through space. But the Bible specifically tells us that this is not the case.

> 2 Corinthians 5:1-5 For we know that if our earthly house, this tent, is destroyed, we have a building from God, a house not made with hands, eternal in the heavens. For in this we groan, earnestly desiring to be clothed with our habitation which is from heaven, if indeed, having been clothed, we shall not be found naked. For we who are in this tent groan, being burdened, not because we want to be unclothed, but further clothed, that mortality may be swallowed up by life.

The writer, the Apostle Paul, says that our souls will not be "naked" in eternity, but that we will have a better body than we have now. He compares the mortal body to a tent and the eternal body to a house. The eternal body is apparently not ghost-like. It is not something misty and insubstantial. The analogy of a tent versus a house would seem to indicate that the eternal body is *more* substantial than the mortal body. It is a body intended to last forever, not just for a few decades.

I tend to think of God taking my soul or my mind out of my current body and dropping it into this new, improved body, like one might get out of a rusty old car and get into a shiny new car. The real "inner" me is the same, but there's a new exterior. But this doesn't appear to be quite what really happens.

> 1 Corinthians 15:35-42, 49-50 But someone will say, "How are the dead raised up? And with what body do they come?" Foolish one, what you sow is not made alive unless it dies. And what you sow, you do not sow that body that shall be, but mere grain — perhaps wheat or some other grain. But God gives it a body as He pleases, and to each seed its own body. All flesh is not the same flesh, but there is one kind of flesh of men, another flesh of animals, another of fish, and another of birds. There are also celestial bodies and terrestrial bodies; but the glory of the celestial is one, and the glory of the terrestrial is another. There is one glory of the sun, another glory of the moon, and another glory of the stars; for one star differs from another star in glory. So also is the resurrection of the dead. The body is sown in corruption, it is raised in incorruption. ... And as we have borne the image of the man of dust, we shall also bear the image of the heavenly Man. Now this I say, brethren, that flesh and blood cannot inherit the kingdom of God; nor does corruption inherit incorruption.

He notes logically enough, that "flesh and blood cannot inherit the kingdom". If we are going to live forever, it stands to reason that we cannot have bodies just like the ones we have now. These bodies wear out, grow old, and die. We will need a different kind of body, a "spiritual body".

But apparently the spiritual body isn't a complete new creation. Paul compares the new body to the plant that grows when you bury a seed: the seed is the old body; the plant is the new body. They don't look much alike, but there's a direct physical connection between them. It's not that some inner essence was plucked out of the seed and placed into the plant. The plant literally came from the seed.

Exactly what does this mean when it comes to our bodies? How will it work? I really have no idea. I don't understand Paul's explanation. Of course it's an analogy, a metaphor, we shouldn't expect the process to be *exactly* like a seed growing into a plant. But how close is the comparison supposed to be?

Note also the very end of the passage quoted above: "We shall also bear the image of the heavenly man". He is talking about the resurrected Christ. Look up just a few verses.

> 1 Corinthians 15:20 But now Christ is risen from the dead, and has become the firstfruits of those who have fallen asleep.

If you read the whole chapter, you will see that Paul is saying that Christ was the first to be resurrected, and that our resurrection will be like his. We can be confident that we will be resurrected because we've seen it already happened once. It's like if a friend offered to repair your car for you and you were nervous that he might not know how to do it right, he might waste your time and whatever money you give him and maybe even make it worse. But if you saw that he had just fixed someone else's car successfully, then you would have some assurance that he can indeed do it. Paul is telling us that we can be sure that God can and will raise us from the dead because he's already done it once, with Christ.

> Phillipians 3:20-21 For our citizenship is in heaven, from which we also eagerly wait for the Savior, the Lord Jesus Christ, who will transform our lowly body that it may be conformed to His glorious body, according to the working by which He is able even to subdue all things to Himself.

Our resurrected bodies will be like Christ's resurrected body. Maybe not exactly the same, because we are not God made man. But his human body was to all appearances just like an ordinary human body, and his resurrected body will be at least very much like our resurrected bodies.

So what was Christ's resurrected body like?

On at least two occasions after his resurrection, Jesus was confused for someone else.

> John 20: 14-15 Now when she [Mary Magdalene] had said this, she turned around and saw Jesus standing there, and did not know that it was Jesus. Jesus said to her, "Woman, why are you weeping? Whom are you seeking?" She, supposing Him to be the gardener, said to Him, "Sir, if You have carried Him away, tell me where You have laid Him, and I will take Him away."

Mary Magdalene saw Jesus, but she didn't recognize him, and she thought he must be the gardener.

> Luke 24:13-16 Now behold, two of them were traveling that same day to a village called Emmaus, which was seven miles from Jerusalem. And they talked together of all these things which had happened. So it was, while they conversed and reasoned, that Jesus Himself drew near and went with them. But their eyes were restrained, so that they did not know Him.

Two of Jesus's followers met Jesus on the road, but they didn't recognize him, and thought he was just some random stranger.

This logically leads to two conclusions: (1) That the resurrection body looks just like an ordinary human body; but (2) It doesn't look exactly like it did before the person was resurrected.

We have to be careful here. Especially in the second case, we're specifically told that God "restrained their eyes" so they wouldn't recognize Jesus. Maybe under normal circumstances they would have recognized him, but God performed a minor miracle to prevent this. There's no mention of God deliberately preventing Mary Magdalene from recognizing Jesus, but maybe he did there too.

Also, these people all knew that Jesus was dead, and were not expecting a resurrection. They didn't expect to see him walking around. My father is dead. If I saw someone on the street who looked just like my father, I doubt I would say, "It's my father come back to life!" It's far more likely I would say, "Huh, what a coincidence, that person looks a lot like my father."

But at the least, these two sections tell us that the resurrection body looks like a normal person. When people saw Jesus after his resurrection, they didn't stare in awe. Nor did they scream and run away. Apparently his body was not glowing or misty or transparent. He didn't have wings or a halo floating over his head. He certainly didn't look like some bizarre monster or science fiction alien. He just looked like a normal person.

Jesus appears to his disciples, and then:

> Luke 24:37-39 But they were terrified and frightened, and supposed they had seen a spirit. And He said to them, "Why are you troubled? And why do doubts arise in your hearts? Behold My hands and My feet, that it is I Myself. Handle Me and see, for a spirit does not have flesh and

bones as you see I have." When He had said this, He showed them His hands and His feet. But while they still did not believe for joy, and marveled, He said to them, "Have you any food here?" So they gave Him a piece of a broiled fish and some honeycomb. And He took it and ate in their presence.

So his body could be touched and felt. And he could eat food. But it certainly was not an ordinary, mortal body.

The verse just before the section I quoted above says:

Luke 24:36 Now as they said these things, Jesus Himself stood in the midst of them, and said to them, "Peace to you."

As the apostle John tells it:

John 20:19 Then, the same day at evening, being the first day of the week, when the doors were shut where the disciples were assembled, for fear of the Jews, Jesus came and stood in the midst, and said to them, "Peace be with you."

So they were in a locked room, and suddenly Jesus appeared. Either he could walk through walls, or he could teleport into the middle of a locked room.

The account of Jesus meeting two men on the road to Emmaus that I quoted earlier ends like this:

Luke 24:31 Then their eyes were opened and they knew Him; and He vanished from their sight.

So he could not only appear at will, he could also disappear.

If you think about it, if you had an immortal body, but could not pass through walls, that could lead to some problems. What if you are trapped under a rockslide or locked in a room or some such in a remote place where no one is around to help you? Could you be stuck there for centuries? Well, maybe in eternity God would rescue you one way or another.

John 20:24-27 Now Thomas, called the Twin, one of the twelve, was not with them when Jesus came. The other disciples therefore said to him, "We have seen the Lord." So he said to them, "Unless I see in His hands the print of the nails, and put my finger into the print of the nails, and put my hand into His side, I will not believe." And after eight days His disciples were again inside, and Thomas with them. Jesus came, the doors being shut, and stood in the midst, and said, "Peace to you!" Then He said to Thomas, "Reach your finger here, and look at My hands; and reach your hand here, and put it into My side. Do not be unbelieving, but believing."

Jesus body still had the fatal wounds that had killed him. It was even possible for someone to put their hand into his side where he had been stabbed with a spear. But he was alive and walking around.

Does this mean that every scar and injury we have picked up on earth will still be present in our eternal bodies? Or was this a special case: Jesus wanted to prove to Thomas that he was really the same man that he had seen killed. I rather doubt that we retain earthly injuries through all eternity. If someone lost his legs on earth, I don't think he goes through eternity with no legs. For that matter, the bodies of most of the people who have died have rotted away by now. I really doubt that in Eternity they are skeletons or less. But clearly injuries that would be fatal to our earthly bodies are not fatal to our eternal bodies, because our eternal bodies cannot die.

Recall that Revelation mentions the tree of life in New Jerusalem:

Revelation 22:2 In the middle of its street, and on either side of the river, was the tree of life, which bore twelve fruits, each tree yielding its fruit every month. The leaves of the tree were for the healing of the nations.

Maybe, possibly this means that if someone's eternal body is injured, they can go to the tree of life and be healed. This isn't the image I have of how an eternal body works. I picture it as being invulnerable to injury. But maybe.

So summing up:

The resurrection body is called a "spiritual body", but it is not ghost-like or insubstantial, but real and concrete. It looks like an ordinary human body and can be touched and felt. It is capable of eating. But it can walk through walls. And of course it lasts forever, and is unhurt by injuries.

That's not a lot. It leaves many questions. But it gives us a few clues.

8.13. Do we become angels?

One of the key elements of the popular view of Heaven is that "good people" became angels when they die.

As we discussed in the previous section, we do get a new "spiritual body" in eternity. But nowhere does it say that we become angels. Perhaps angels have "spiritual bodies" too, but nothing says that our bodies will be like those of angels. Indeed, if you refer back to 1 Corinthians 15, you may note that the writer, Paul, carefully points out that just as there are different kinds of physical bodies – humans are different from dogs and monkeys and so on – there are also different kinds of spiritual bodies.

Nowhere in the Bible is an angel connected to a formerly living person. We are never told that the "angel of David" came back to speak to someone or anything like that. In the few cases where the spirit of a dead person did come back – such as when Moses and Elijah appeared on the "mount of transfiguration", Matthew 17:1-13 -- they are not described or referred to as being angels.

The only connection the Bible gives between resurrected people and angels is this:

> Matthew 22: 30 For in the resurrection they neither marry nor are given in marriage, but are like angels of God in heaven.

Note it says that after the resurrection, the saved will be "like the angels". Not "will *be* angels" but will be "*like* angels". In context this isn't saying that the saved will be like angels in general, but only in one specific way: that, like angels, they won't marry.

One additional indication that we won't become angels:

> 1 Corinthians 6:3 Do you not know that we shall judge angels? How much more, things that pertain to this life?

We will at some point apparently be above the angels. We won't be angels, we'll be ruling over angels. Though I suppose that angels might judge other angels, so this isn't definitive.

So where does the idea come from? I suspect that it just comes from some lazy thinking: angels are in Heaven, people will be in Heaven, therefore people will become angels.

There is no reason to believe that people become angels after they die.

8.14. Will we work in eternity?

The common picture of Heaven often depicts the saints lying around on clouds. Their only activity appears to be strumming harps. Is there work in Paradise? Or is it a period of eternal relaxation?

There are some Bible verses that talk about rest in Paradise. The most notable and oft-quoted is:

> Hebrews 4:9-10 There remains therefore a rest for the people of God. For he who has entered His rest has himself also ceased from his works as God did from His.

Others verses indicate that there is work to be done in Paradise. Speaking of the New Jerusalem, Revelation says:

> Revelation 22:3 … the throne of God and of the Lamb shall be in it, and His servants shall serve Him.

In another place, Jesus tells a parable about the Kingdom of Heaven:

> Matthew 25:14-23 "For the kingdom of heaven is like a man traveling to a far country, who called his own servants and delivered his goods to them. And to one he gave five talents, to another two, and to another one, to each according to his own ability; and immediately he went on a journey. Then he who had received the five talents went and traded with them, and made another five talents. And likewise he who had received two gained two more also. But he who had received one went and dug in the ground, and hid his lord's money. After a long time the lord of those servants came and settled accounts with them. So he who had received five talents came and brought five other talents, saying, 'Lord, you delivered to me five talents; look, I have gained five more talents besides them.' His lord said to him, 'Well done, good and faithful servant; you were faithful over a few things, I will make you ruler over many things. Enter into the joy of your lord.' He also who had received two talents came and said, 'Lord, you delivered to me two talents; look, I have gained two more talents besides them.' His lord said to him, 'Well done, good and faithful servant; you have been faithful over a few things, I will make you ruler over many things. Enter into the joy of your lord.'

If you read the whole parable, the point is that those who squander the talents God has given them will be punished and those who use their talents effectively will be rewarded.

Side note: The "talent" in the parable is a unit of money. The boss trusts each of his employees with various amounts of money. The point of the parable is that God entrusts each of us with all sorts of things, not just money but skills and, well, talents – and that he will judge us on how well we use these things. It is, in fact, from this parable that we get our modern English word "talent". Bible teachers would say things like, "So what talents has God trusted you with?", referring to the money in the parable but meaning skills and abilities, and the word "talent" came to mean skills and abilities.

Anyway, the point of the parable is that God will reward his servants based on how they use the talents he has given them. But note the nature of the reward: "You have been faithful over a few things, I will make you ruler over many things." The reward for doing a good job is ... more responsibility and more work!

Similarly, we discussed in section 6.14 that there are some parallels between Eden and New Jerusalem. New Jerusalem may be the fulfillment of what Eden was meant to become. In any case, Eden was the first Paradise, the world the way God intended it to be.

So in Eden, were people on a permanent vacation? No. Adam was expected to work.

Genesis 2:15 Then the Lord God took the man and put him in the garden of Eden to tend and keep it.

Adam's first job was to take care of the garden.
A little less directly:

Genesis 1:28 Then God blessed them, and God said to them, "Be fruitful and multiply; fill the earth and subdue it; have dominion over the fish of the sea, over the birds of the air, and over every living thing that moves on the earth."

Humans were given the job of ruling over the Earth God created, to "subdue" it and "have dominion over" it. Christian thinkers have taken this to be a mandate for everything from science to industry to environmentalism. We could debate exactly what it means and how broad it is, but if it means anything at all, it means that humans have the right to use the Earth and animals for our own purposes, and the responsibility to do this wisely and well.

If there was work in the paradise of Eden, it is plausible to suppose that there will be work in the paradise of New Jerusalem.

It is not difficult to reconcile the verses about rest with the verses about work and responsibility. There could be both. On Earth we have both work and rest, there's no reason to suppose that we can't have both in Paradise.

Personally, while I like a nice vacation, I think a life of one long vacation would get pretty boring pretty fast. Yes, sometimes I like to just lie down and snooze. But I also like to do something useful now and then. I think most people get satisfaction from a job well done, whether it's something dramatic like travelling to the moon or something simple like cleaning the floor.

I'd guess that work in Paradise will never be drudgery but will always be rewarding and satisfying. It might be long and hard, but it won't be pointless and tiresome.

8.15. Is there private property in eternity?

Micah 4 describes a time when God reigns on Earth.

Micah 4:1,3-5 In the last days the mountain of the Lord's temple will be established as the highest of the mountains; it will be exalted above the hills, and peoples will stream to it. … He will judge between many peoples and will settle disputes for strong nations far and wide. They will beat their swords into plowshares and their spears into pruning hooks. Nation will not take up sword against nation, nor will they train for war anymore. Everyone will sit under their own vine and under their own fig tree, and no one will make them afraid, for the Lord Almighty has spoken. All the nations may walk in the name of their gods, but we will walk in the name of the Lord our God for ever and ever. (NIV)

This is a prophecy about Eternity, and not about some "ordinary" time of more peace and prosperity, because it says not only that people will not fight, but they will not "train for war anymore", and that this period will last "for ever and ever". This language may be poetic, but it appears to be literal. This is not a passing period of peace in the ups and downs of history.

So note that in the description of this time of divine grace and peace, we are told, "everyone shall sit under their own vine and under their own fig tree".

So God's idea of paradise is not that private property is abolished and we all share everything in a utopian communist state, but that everyone can enjoy his own property free from fear of it being stolen, destroyed, or vandalized.

Logically, I take it for granted that in Paradise people do not greedily horde wealth, exploit others, and force them to live in poverty, while God stands by and does nothing. But one can certainly imagine a society where people value their own property while respecting that of others.

By the way, nowhere in the Bible does God say that we should not enjoy material things.

> Ecclesiastes 2:24 Nothing is better for a man than that he should eat and drink, and that his soul should enjoy good in his labor. This also, I saw, was from the hand of God.

God wants us to enjoy the good things that he has given us, or given us the ability to create from the raw materials that he has given us – food and drink and clothes and houses and good books and ice cream and video games. These things are gifts from God. He wouldn't have created them if he hadn't intended for us to enjoy them.

People often have the mistaken idea that the problem with greed is that the greedy person gets too much pleasure from material things. This is exactly backwards. The problem with greed is that the greedy person does not get enough pleasure from material things. Instead of enjoying the things that God has given him, he always wants something else. No matter how much he has, it is never enough. He never enjoys the things he has because he is constantly consumed with getting more. Instead of enjoying what God has given him, and being thankful to God and praising God for all these good things, he complains that God hasn't given him enough. God gives him a present, and he spits in God's face and says, "It's not good enough."

8.16. Are people in Paradise free?

There is no sin in Paradise. So when we go to Paradise, does God judge sin quickly and harshly? That doesn't seem to make sense. That would make Paradise a place of strict laws and toughn penalties. The idea of beatings or prison doesn't fit with the idea of a place of joy.

So most theologians assume that God will take away our desire to sin, so that the issue never comes up. But if that's the case, then isn't

God taking away our freedom? And how can a place be Paradise if there is no freedom, but everyone is obliged to obey a long list of laws as a mindless robot? It sounds more like a totalitarian nightmare than Paradise.

Indeed, this is an objection that many atheists have to Christianity. Why would I want to go to a Heaven, they ask, where I have to obey all these rules?

But this thinking assumes that people in Paradise really want to sin. Christians do not really want to sin.

Romans 7:15 For what I am doing, I do not understand. For what I will to do, that I do not practice; but what I hate, that I do.

Does this verse sound like your own experience? It certainly does for me. You commit some sin. You see how it is ruining your relationships with family or friends, maybe endangering your job, maybe even getting you in trouble with the law. It certainly sours your fellowship with God. Maybe you even hate yourself for doing it. You swear you will never do it again. And then you do it again.

All Christians struggle against temptation. We don't want to fall to it. We want to overcome it. So by taking away temptation, God is not taking away our freedom, but rather giving us the ability to do what we really want to do.

"Freedom" does not mean the absence of obligation, but rather the ability to choose when we want to be obligated and when we don't and what obligations we will take on. For example, when two people marry, they are making all sorts of commitments to each other. In a free society, each person will have the right to marry whomever they want and who will have them. A society where the government told you whom you must marry would certainly not be what we would call a free society. But a society that made marriage illegal would not be a free society either. Just the opposite, I think most human beings would agree that any government that banned marriage was a tyranny. People *want* to commit to each other in marriage. They want to give up the freedom to become romantically involved with other people, while their husband or wife makes the same commitment to them. A society that said, "We don't want you to be limited to one romantic partner for the rest of your life, therefore we will forbid you from making this commitment" would not be more free. It would be less free.

Similarly, when you get a job, you are promising to do certain work in exchange for pay. A society that banned employment would not be a free society. A society that said, "No one should be obligated to work in exchange for money, therefore we will ban all contracts" would not be more free. It would be less free. (Presumably it would also be a very poor society very quickly. But that's another issue.)

Freedom is the right to choose for yourself what commitments you will make, not the absence of any commitments. People who enter Paradise *want* to be freed from temptation. They will gladly make a commitment to never sin again in exchange for the ability to live up to that commitment.

Of course there are many people in the world who do not want to make such a commitment. They enjoy sin, or think that any day now they will find a sin that they can truly enjoy. Such people will not be admitted into Paradise, because they don't meet the most basic requirements to go there. They don't want what's there. While the suffering in Hell will be terrible, they prefer to suffer in Hell to having to give up their "right" to sin.

By the way, there is not a long list of rules in Paradise. The Bible celebrates freedom of thought and conscience. For example, in the early church there was a controversy about what food Christians should eat. The Apostle Paul replied that on such disputable matters each person should decide for himself and not try to impose his opinions on others.

1 Corinthians 10:29b-30 For why is my freedom being judged by another's conscience? If I take part in the meal with thankfulness, why am I denounced because of something I thank God for? (NIV)

How many commandments did God give to Moses? Only ten. Jesus said that we only need two laws: "Love the Lord your God with all your heart, with all your soul, and with all your mind," and "Love your neighbor as yourself." (Matthew 22:37-40) You can fit the laws God wants people to follow on a single sheet of paper. Compare that to men's laws. According to the Government Printing Office, the laws and regulations about taxes alone -- "Title 26" of the Federal Code -- take up 16,845 pages.

8.17. Where are we between death and resurrection?

Where are we between the time that we die, and when we are with Christ? There are several theories:

(1) When we die we immediately go to be with Christ with a glorified body.

(2) When we die our souls immediately go to be with Christ. We do not get a new body until some time later, at the resurrection.

(3) We are not conscious between death and resurrection. At death we enter "soul sleep". We wake up at the resurrection. (Note: This is not the same as the "soul sleep" taught by Seventh Day Adventists. What we're talking about here is temporary; what Seventh Day Adventists talk about is permanent. See section 8.4.)

(4) Eternity is not governed by the same time as Earth – it is a whole different "time zone". When we die we immediately go to be with Christ, but how this relates to events happening on Earth is complex.

Biblical and logical arguments can be made to support all of these theories.

1 Corinthians 15: 51-54 Behold, I tell you a mystery: We shall not all sleep, but we shall all be changed — in a moment, in the twinkling of an eye, at the last trumpet. For the trumpet will sound, and the dead will be raised incorruptible, and we shall be changed. For this corruptible must put on incorruption, and this mortal must put on immortality. So when this corruptible has put on incorruption, and this mortal has put on immortality, then shall be brought to pass the saying that is written: "Death is swallowed up in victory."

This seems to say that the resurrection is a future event. Most people will "sleep" until the resurrection, though those who are alive at the time of the resurrection will get their glorified bodies without ever entering this sleep state. (Exactly when this will happen gets into prophecy, which I'm trying to avoid doing.)

Likewise:

Revelation 20:4b-5 Then I saw the souls of those who had been beheaded for their witness to Jesus and for the word of God, who had not worshiped the beast or his image, and had not received his mark on their foreheads or on their hands. And they lived and reigned with Christ for a thousand years. But the rest of the dead did not live again until the thousand years were finished. This is the first resurrection.

Again, this pretty clearly says that the resurrection is a specific event that will happen some time in the future. There will be two resurrections: the first resurrection for a small group of particularly holy or blessed people, and the second resurrection for everyone else, 1000 years apart.

On the other hand:

2 Corinthians 5:6,8 So we are always confident, knowing that while we are at home in the body we are absent from the Lord. ... We are confident, yes, well pleased rather to be absent from the body and to be present with the Lord.

This seems to be saying that once you are no longer in your body, you are present with Christ, that there is no intermediate stage. Similarly:

Phillipians 1:21-23 For to me, to live is Christ, and to die is gain. But if I live on in the flesh, this will mean fruit from my labor; yet what I shall choose I cannot tell. For I am hard-pressed between the two, having a desire to depart and be with Christ, which is far better.

One could argue that it doesn't say that the transition is instant: there might be a delay between leaving the body and being present with Christ.

When Jesus was crucified, two thieves were crucified at the same time.

Luke 23:42-43 Then he said to Jesus, "Lord, remember me when You come into Your kingdom." And Jesus said to him, "Assuredly, I say to you, today you will be with Me in Paradise."

When Christians discuss these verses they usually concentrate on the nature of repentance and forgiveness that this conveys. The thief confessed his guilt in the previous few verses (before what I just quoted). There is no question of him being a good man who was wrongly accused. He is going to be dead within hours, so he will have no opportunity to do good works to make up for his past crimes. And yet Jesus tells him that he will be admitted into Paradise. Salvation is by faith, not by works.

But for our purposes here I want to focus on one word: "today". Jesus did not say, "Thousands of years from now I will come again, and then there will be a resurrection, and then you will be with me in Paradise." No, he said "today". It's hard to see how to read this verse without concluding that immediately after we die, or at least within a few hours, we are conscious and with Christ.

I suppose one could argue that Jesus is simplifying. He and the thief were both in incredible pain. Maybe this wasn't the time for an extended discussion of the details. But still, if there is a gap in time before the dead enter Paradise, why would Jesus say "today"? Why wouldn't he have just said, "Someday you will be with me in Paradise", or "The next thing you will know is waking up in Paradise", etc?

Previously we have discussed the story of Lazarus and the rich man, Luke 16:19-31. (Section 6.12.) We need not go over it again. But let's just note one thing: The rich man was in Hades, and apparently conscious and talking, and Lazarus was in "Abraham's Bosom", at the time Jesus was on this Earth or earlier. So again, it seems that people are conscious and either with Christ or in Hades now. This is not something that will wait until the future.

One way we might reconcile these verses is to theorize that the resurrection is not a single, future event, but that each believer is resurrected immediately when he dies.

But this doesn't seem to be consistent with Revelation 20, quoted above. That clearly says that there are two resurrections, one group resurrected first and "the rest of the dead" resurrected later. There are not millions of resurrections, one for each person. Just two.

One could say that these two resurrections are not in the future, but that the events described are past. Some people believe that the thousand years began sometime after John wrote Revelation, but before our own time, and so the prophecy is now fulfilled.

But that doesn't really help. John says the second resurrection will not happen "until the thousand years were finished". So for at least a thousand years after John's time, people were not being resurrected. All the "immediate" verses I have quoted were written before Revelation – most scholars say that Revelation was the last book of the Bible to be written. So if there's a contradiction between the "immediate" verses and the "future" verses, such a theory only resolves it for people who die a thousand years or more after the Bible was written.

And then we have to wonder what happens to people who die after this thousand years is over. If all the "rest of the dead" are resurrected after the thousand years, and then history continues, what happens to those who die after that? Is there a third resurrection?

The best resolution to my mind is to suppose that when we die, we immediately go to be with Christ, but we don't immediately get our glorified bodies. In between our deaths and the resurrection, we are living in some intermediate state. Then at the resurrection we get our glorified bodies. Perhaps in the meantime we are bodiless souls, or in some other state.

A catch to this is that the Bible doesn't mention any intermediate state. We have to completely invent the concept just to reconcile these verses. So I'm not totally satisfied with this solution, but it's the only thing I have heard or can think of that fits.

8.18. Temple in heaven

When the Jews built the temple to God, they didn't hire an architect to design it. God gave specific instructions what the temple was supposed to be like, including the floor plan, the building materials, and detailed descriptions of the furnishings.

This temple was modeled after a temple in Heaven. That is, there is an "original" temple in Heaven, and the temple on Earth was a copy of this.

Exodus 25:8-9 And let them make Me a sanctuary, that I may dwell among them. According to all that I show you, that is, the pattern of the tabernacle and the pattern of all its furnishings, just so you shall make it.

God gave Moses the "pattern" for the temple and the furnishings. He didn't leave it to Moses to come up with a design on his own.

Revelation 11:19a Then the temple of God was opened in heaven, and the ark of His covenant was seen in His temple.

Revelation 15:5 After these things I looked, and behold, the temple of the tabernacle of the testimony in heaven was opened.

Revelation 8:3 mentions an altar but does not specifically mention a temple.

Thus, there are several mentions in Revelation of there being a temple in Heaven. There's no real description of it or explanation of its relationship to the temple on Earth; it's just mentioned as being there.

But Hebrews indicates that there is a relationship.

> Hebrews 8:4-5 For if He [Jesus] were on earth, He would not be a priest, since there are priests who offer the gifts according to the law; who serve the copy and shadow of the heavenly things, as Moses was divinely instructed when he was about to make the tabernacle. For He said, "See that you make all things according to the pattern shown you on the mountain."

> Hebrews 9:11-12 But Christ came as High Priest of the good things to come, with the greater and more perfect tabernacle not made with hands, that is, not of this creation. Not with the blood of goats and calves, but with His own blood He entered the Most Holy Place once for all, having obtained eternal redemption.

> Hebrews 9:23-24 Therefore it was necessary that the copies of the things in the heavens should be purified with these, but the heavenly things themselves with better sacrifices than these. For Christ has not entered the holy places made with hands, which are copies of the true, but into heaven itself, now to appear in the presence of God for us;

The most plain reading of these sections is that there is a temple in Heaven, and that the temple on Earth is a copy of this temple in Heaven. That is, God gave Moses the floor plan and design of the temple in Heaven and Moses was supposed to make a copy of this temple on Earth. Perhaps this was to give people on Earth at least a small picture of Heaven. We are told that certain elements of the temple are symbols to remind us of the nature of God and our relationship to him. Maybe everything about the temple is important in some way, and so it is, in a million ways big and small, the most appropriate environment in which to worship God, whether in Heaven or on Earth.

This may be an excessively mundane analogy, but: Fast food chains have figured out very efficient ways to make hamburgers or chicken sandwiches or whatever in a certain style. So when they open a new restaurant, they build it exactly according to the existing pattern.

There's no point starting over from scratch trying to figure out what equipment to have and where to put it. They make the new restaurant just like the existing, highly-successful ones.

Others read this as saying that Christ is the perfect "temple", and that the temple on Earth was a "copy" in the sense that it was full of symbols pointing to Christ. That is, it is not a copy in the sense of being another building built from the same blueprints, but that it is a building that symbolizes Christ. It's like we build monuments to people that we respect. No one supposes that the Washington Monument looks anything like George Washington. It's not a statue of the man. It's a symbol.

But nowhere does the writer of Hebrews say that the temple is a symbol for Christ or that it is "like Christ". He says that it is a copy of the temple in Heaven. Indeed, he says that Christ entered the Heavenly temple. If the Heavenly temple is a symbol of Christ, than he is saying that Christ entered himself. So I find this theory unlikely.

The writer of Hebrews was probably familiar with Greek philosophy. The Greek philosopher Plato had written that he believed that everything on Earth was a poor reflection or copy of "perfect forms" that existed only in some mystical place. That is, somewhere there was, say, the perfect dog, and the dogs we see on Earth are all just imperfect copies of that perfect dog. This idea is sometimes called "Platonic forms". A dog could be a good dog if it was very similar to the perfect dog, and a bad dog if it was less like the perfect dog.

Some suggest, then, that the writer of Hebrews was alluding to or borrowing from Greek philosophy. To the Greeks, ideas like this were the latest and most advanced science. They talked about Plato's forms much like 21st century Americans talk about relativity or black holes: it's the latest idea from the smartest people, and most people probably really don't understand it, but they'll toss it into their conversation thinking that the principles behind it may apply here, or maybe just to make themselves sound smart. So, the thinking goes, the writer of Hebrews may have tossed this Greek philosophy into his writing to make it sound modern and appealing to his audience.

I'm sure an atheist would say that the writer just copied the trendy ideas of his day and "re-interpreted" scripture in light of what was then "modern science", like some 21st century Christians try to fit the Bible to the latest scientific or pseudo-scientific fad. But if that's true, then this part of the Bible, at least, is not inspired by God but is mere human wisdom.

But just because the Bible happens to coincide with a popular idea doesn't mean that the Bible writers stole the idea from popular culture. In this case, the writer does not specifically mention Plato, so if he is trying to relate Christianity to Greek philosophy, he is not spelling it out. The writer may be alluding to Plato but doesn't want to make the connection explicit because he doesn't want the reader to think he is endorsing everything Plato wrote. Or the similarity may just be a coincidence.

I tend to think it's just a coincidence, though the similarity is just too striking for me to say this confidently.

In any case, the important point is, there is a temple in Heaven, and the temple on Earth is a copy of this.

9. Conclusions

So let's wrap it all up. Here are my conclusions.

9.1. The popular view, revisited

Now that we've studied what the Bible actually has to say about Eternity, we can see how far off the popular view is.

"Good people go to Heaven when they die." Wrong on two counts. First, no one goes to Heaven when they die: the saved go to Paradise or New Jerusalem. Second, you don't get there by being good: you get there by accepting Christ as your savior.

"Bad people go to Hell." Partly right. The unsaved go to Hell, but they are not necessarily any worse than the people who go to Paradise. They are the people who have not accepted Christ's offer of forgiveness for their sins.

"Saint Peter sits at the entrance to Heaven and looks up each person in a big book to see if he should be admitted." No and yes. Nowhere does the Bible say that Saint Peter sits at the gates of either Heaven or Paradise. It says that angels stand at the gates, not Peter. It does say that there is a "Book of Life". Revelation 20:15 says that anyone whose name is *not* in the Book of Life is thrown into the lake of fire, and Revelation 22:19 says that anyone whose name *is* written in the Book of Life is admitted into New Jerusalem.

"People become angels when they die." No, they don't.

"In Eternity people have wings, float around on clouds, and play harps." Wrong, wrong, and okay, at least some do. Nowhere does the Bible say that the new bodies the saved will be given have wings. As Jesus resurrected body appears to be the model for the new bodies we will get, and people mistook him for an ordinary man, it seems very unlikely that he had wings. There is no mention of floating around on clouds. We'll be living in a city. There are a few mentions in Revelation of the saved in Eternity playing harps: Revelation 5:8, but this refers to a specific group of 24 people, not all the saved. In Revelation 14:2 John says he hears the sound of harps, but doesn't say who is playing them. Revelation 15:2 says that those who were killed during the Great Tribulation at the end of the age were given harps. Again, not all the saved, and no indication that playing these harps was all they did for the rest of time.

"Heaven has streets of gold and pearly gates." Basically true. If we substitute "New Jerusalem" for "Heaven", Revelation 21 says that New Jerusalem has a street or town square of gold and 12 gates each made of a single pearl.

"The Devil has red skin, horns and a tail, and carries a pitch fork." No, he doesn't.

"The Devil rules Hell." No, he's not the ruler there, he's a prisoner.

Most elements of the popular view of Eternity are simply wrong. Or at least, they do not come from the Bible. One could trace where these ideas came from historically, but that would be a different book.

9.2. Things I'm fairly sure of

When the Bible speaks of Heaven, it uses the word in three ways: (1) The sky, (2) Space, (3) God's throne. But there is no indication that the saved will live there.

The place where the saved will live is the New Jerusalem, also called Paradise. This will be a huge city, probably traveling in orbit around the Earth.

But not around our current Earth. At some point in the future, God will destroy this present Earth, burning up the very atoms that make it up, and will create a new Earth for the saved to live on.

The unsaved will be sent to Hell, which is a place of fire, darkness, and suffering. We can debate exactly what it is like, but it is clearly an unpleasant place to live.

New Jerusalem is not yet ready. In the meantime, the dead live in Sheol, also called Hades. This is some sort of intermediate place, the "waiting room". Sheol has a pleasant part, "Abraham's Bosom", for the saved, and an unpleasant part for the unsaved. At some time in the future, God will destroy Sheol. The saved will then go to Paradise, and the unsaved will be sent to Hell, also called the Lake of Fire, and Gehenna.

The Kingdom of Heaven is not a place but a group of people, those who follow God. The Kingdom of Heaven exists today and will continue to exist forever.

In Eternity we will have new, "glorified" bodies. These bodies will resemble our present bodies: they will have two arms and two legs and generally look human. They will be physical bodies: we won't be ghost-like, but will be able to eat and drink and touch each other and so on. But these new bodies will last forever, they will be capable of moving through walls, and probably other abilities that we do not presently have.

9.3.   Things that are more debatable

We will not spend all of our time in New Jerusalem: it has gates that are open all the time so we can come and go. So I suspect that we will be exploring and filling the universe. There's a big universe out there – billions of galaxies each with billions of suns, probably billions of planets. We'll have all of time to settle all this space, and we'll need it.

Maybe this is what Jesus meant when he said:

Matthew 5:5 Blessed are the meek, For they shall inherit the earth.

The meek may inherit the Earth because the bold will leave to explore the rest of the universe.

(If that sounds too much like science fiction, bear in mind that if you told someone a thousand years ago that someday the Gospel would come to a far away continent that they have never seen called "America", and that the people of this continent would send missionaries all over the world in metal flying machines, that would have sounded like a fantasy story, too.)

We won't spend our time just floating around on clouds playing harps. We'll be working and building.

I've sometimes heard Christians say that they hope Jesus doesn't return too soon because there are all these things they want to do before the world ends: businessmen and engineers want to finish some big project, young women want to get married, etc. This only makes sense if you assume that Paradise will be boring. But surely God would not plan for us to spend eternity being bored.

When God created the universe and human beings, he had a wonderful plan for people to live in perfect fellowship with him. He commanded people to be fruitful and multiply and to conquer the Earth. But then people sinned and trashed God's plan. We have now spent thousands of years on a disastrous wrong turn. Someday Christ will return and set everything right, and then God will restart his perfect plan and get us back on track. The Second Coming will not be the end of human civilization. It will be the beginning. Humanity set off on a journey, but when we stepped out the door we headed the wrong way down the street. When we finally get turned around and pointed in the right direction, would you say that at that point the journey is over? Of course not. At that point it is just beginning.

The Bible does not give a lot of detail about what we will be doing in Eternity. We probably wouldn't understand it. But whatever it is, it will be far more satisfying and exciting and just plain fun than anything we are doing today.

On the other hand, Hell is a place of horror and torment. What makes it terrible is primarily that it is a place of complete separation from God. People there will be free to do whatever they want, unbound by God's law or any restraint from the Holy Spirit. And they will use that freedom just like people on Earth have always used freedom from God's laws: to ruin their own lives and the lives of everyone around them. Here on Earth people routinely announce that they are throwing off the shackles of primitive superstitions like Christianity to build an atheist, humanist utopia. And they usually end up with drug abuse, sexual perversion, slavery, torture, and genocide. I don't know if exactly those same forms of depravity will exist in Hell. Presumably people can't murder each other in Hell, as they will all live forever. But they will find similar things. Hell will be like Nero's Rome or Nazi Germany or North Korea, times a thousand.

9.4. More speculative

You may recall way back in section 6.14 we noted that there are some parallels between Eden and New Jerusalem. This leads me to a theory: New Jerusalem will be what Eden was intended to become. Or to put it another way, New Jerusalem will be what life on Earth would be like if people had never sinned. Or to put it a third way, New Jerusalem will be just like Earth is today, except with no sin.

Of course that's a big "except"! It's a little like saying that a place is just like the ocean but with no water.

Our lives today are dominated by sin – our own sins and the sins of others. And I'm not just talking about drug addicts and criminals, but all of us.

Think of all the things you do to protect yourself from the effects of sin. For example, every time I step out the front door of my house, the next thing I do is I turn around and lock the door behind me. Why? To make it a little harder for criminals to break in and steal my things or harm my family.

Most of us avoid certain parts of town, especially after dark. We keep our money in the bank rather than at home, at least partly to protect it from thieves. We routinely use passwords on computer accounts and run virus checkers on our computers.

A substantial portion of our income goes to taxes. Some of those taxes go for things that would exist in a perfect world, like maintaining roads. But a chunk goes to police to protect us from criminals, and armies to protect us from foreign tyrants. Another chunk goes to corrupt bureaucrats and various payoffs.

Et cetera.

What would a world with no sin be like? Some things are obvious.

There would be no armies. No one would be launching a war of aggression, and if there are no aggressors, then there is no need to defend yourself from them.

If police departments continued to exist, they would be very different from what they are now. There would be no crime so there'd be no need to protect people from crime. They might still perform administrative functions, like directing traffic and managing crowds. Will there be accidents in Paradise? We might still have something like police to clean up after accidents. Presumably no one could be killed in an accident as they all have immortal bodies. But will people still run into each other and damage property? Most accidents are not caused by sin.

There would be no drug abuse or drunkenness or gluttony. People would enjoy the food and drink God gives us, but always in moderation.

I suppose people might still have locks on doors as a way to prevent others from accidentally walking in when they want privacy. But there would be no need for truly secure locks or alarm systems.

There are things that we do on Earth that will not be done in Paradise because they will be unnecessary there. For example, there will be no funeral homes or morticians, because we will all have immortal bodies. Well, in a sense, this too is because of the absence of sin: death exists because of the curse God placed on Adam, and God made that curse because of sin. In New Jerusalem, the curse is ended, so there is no more death.

I have said that I conclude from scripture that people still work in Paradise. In Eden, Adam was supposed to tend the garden. People will still eat and drink – Jesus made a point of eating after his resurrection, and he said that he would drink wine with us in Paradise – so it is likely there is still farming and gardening in Paradise. Revelation mentions people wearing white robes and playing harps. Does God create these things miraculously, or does someone make them?

I suspect that we will build and make things in Paradise just like we do here on Earth. And if people are building and making things, it seems likely that they will trade things they have made with each other. I, for example, enjoy developing computer software, but I hate carpentry. There are plenty of people in the world who are the opposite. I suppose God could change us so that we all love every possible activity. But that would take away our personalities. Why would he do that? I assume he would take away sinful desires, but not wholesome ones. So if I enjoy developing computer software and someone else enjoys building things from wood, it makes sense that we would trade the product of our labor, even in Paradise. (Okay, I'm assuming that there are computers in Paradise. But what sort of Paradise would it be without computer games?)

This brings us to the classic story economists tell of how money was invented. Suppose Al makes birdhouses and wants a cherry pie, and Betty makes cherry pies and wants a birdhouse. So Al can make an extra birdhouse and Betty can make an extra cherry pie and they trade and both are happy. But suppose Al makes birdhouses and wants a cherry pie, and Betty makes cherry pies but what she wants right now is a bicycle. They can't trade because Al has nothing Betty wants. Maybe they can find a third person, lets call him Carl, who makes bicycles and wants a birdhouse. Then Al could give Carl a birdhouse, Carl could give Betty a bicycle, and Betty could give Al a cherry pie. But this is getting complicated, and in real life it could get much more complicated. Maybe in Paradise this isn't an issue. Maybe people work because the work is satisfying and they just give the products of their work away, and no one is lazy or tries to take advantage of others. Or maybe in Paradise they have the same solution we have here on Earth: have a single product that everyone recognizes as having value, so you can always trade for that product, not because you want that product, but because you know that you can always trade it for what you do want. That's pretty much the definition of money. Will there be money in Paradise? Maybe.

Whether there is money, or some other means for people to share the product of their work, people might still write contracts so that everyone knew exactly what they are agreeing to. But there would never be any fear of someone breaking a contract.

I can't help but wonder: Will there be selling and advertising in Paradise? The idea of billboards in New Jerusalem seems rather incongruous. Is that a rational feeling? Or is that just the product of our reaction to the way advertising on Earth is drenched with deception and greed? That is, maybe we can't imagine advertising in Paradise because we see that on Earth it is so wrapped up in sin. But if it existed in Paradise, it would be perfectly honest. In a sinless world, the purpose of advertising would be to inform people that you have made some product, and where and how to get it, not to trick them into buying junk.

I don't suppose that the question of whether there is advertising in Paradise is all that important, but you can apply this same reasoning to all sorts of things.

If something is inherently sinful, of course it will not exist in Paradise. Likewise if something exists only to protect us from sin, it will be unnecessary. Other things may not relate to sin per se, but will be unnecessary because of the way in which our lives will be different. But I think that most things that we do on Earth that are basically good, things that relate to working and learning and loving each other, will probably still be done in Paradise. Almost everything we do on Earth is tainted by sin in some way, so in Paradise we will have pure forms of these things, not the corrupted form we have here.

Christians are told that we will rule in Paradise and that we will judge angels. There are nations and kings. So there will be some sort of government, and people will still divide themselves up into different countries. Presumably these countries will not go to war with each other. They might have international soccer competitions. Will they be the same countries that exist on Earth today, i.e. will there be a United States and a France and a China and so forth? Bear in mind that this present Earth will be destroyed and God will create a new Earth. The new Earth has no oceans, so it has different geography. It is not a copy of the present Earth. So there can't be countries that occupy the same land that they do here. That land will no longer exist. Perhaps people who were, say, Americans here on this Earth will carve out a piece of land on the New Earth and call it "New America". Or maybe the nations on New Earth will be unrelated to nations on this Earth. Maybe people will group themselves together by criteria that seem more relevant to that time and place.

In any case, the most important point is: Paradise will be a place where we have perfect fellowship with God, and where there is no sin, so people can freely love and trust each other. We will most definitely not be bored. Our lives will be more satisfying, productive, and plain fun than anything we experience on Earth. The best experiences we have on Earth are a shadow of what we will experience in Paradise. In Paradise we will live as God intended us to live. We will fully enjoy all the good things that God has created for us, including material things, natural beauty, love and friendship of other people, satisfying work, and of course, fellowship with God himself.

INDEX

J

Jacob, 36, 61, 63, 128
Jesus, 2, 6, 11, 12, 23, 25, 36, 45, 48, 49,
    51, 52, 54, 58, 60, 61, 62, 63, 64, 68,
    70, 76, 78, 79, 80, 82, 94, 95, 96, 113,
    117, 119, 120, 121, 123, 124, 126,
    127, 128, 129, 130, 131, 134, 135,
    136, 137, 139, 146, 147, 153, 155, 157

K

Kingdom of God, 61, 62, 63, 64
Kingdom of Heaven, 12, 63, 64, 77, 80,
    139, 154
Koran, 68

L

Lake of Fire, 20, 29, 46, 47, 58, 59, 60,
    112, 154
Lazarus, 78, 79, 80, 81, 82, 147
Limbo, 32, 97, 98, 99
Lindsay, Hal, 15
Luther, Martin, 100

M

marriage, 94, 127, 128, 129, 130, 131,
    143
Michael, 57
money, 2, 76, 100, 134, 140, 144, 156,
    158
Mormons, 119, 129, 130
Moses, 68, 80, 138, 148, 149
mythology, 42, 57, 58

N

New Earth, 3, 70, 82, 89
New Heaven, 70, 84
New Jerusalem, 3, 20, 85, 86, 87, 88, 89,
    90, 91, 92, 93, 95, 96, 131, 139, 140,
    141, 152, 153, 154, 156, 158
North Korea, 115, 156
Norway, 29, 30

P

parable, 78, 79, 80, 81, 113, 114, 121,
    123, 139, 140
Paradise, 2, 20, 39, 76, 81, 95, 96, 110,
    118, 119, 122, 124, 125, 126, 127,
    131, 139, 140, 141, 142, 143, 144,
    146, 147, 152, 153, 154, 155, 157,
    158, 159
Paul, 66, 92, 107, 120, 132, 133, 134, 138
pearly gates, 91, 153
Pharisees, 62, 79
Pit, 41, 42
planets, 67, 69, 77, 84, 131, 154
Plato, 44, 83, 150
prison, 47, 53, 54, 55, 58, 79, 118, 119,
    127, 142
Protestants, 57, 115
punishment, 37, 43, 47, 50, 58, 110, 111,
    112, 113, 114, 119, 122, 125, 127
Purgatory, 32, 99, 100

Q

qeber, 35

R

resurrection, 49, 111, 128, 132, 134, 135,
    137, 138, 145, 146, 147, 148, 157
Rome, 87, 156
rules, 24, 114, 117, 118, 121, 143, 144,
    153
Russia, 16, 41, 88

S

Sadducees, 127, 128, 130, 131
Samaria, 12
Satan, 25, 49, 53, 56, 57, 72, 112
Septuagint, 44
Sheol, 32, 33, 34, 35, 36, 37, 38, 39, 40,
    41, 42, 43, 44, 45, 46, 52, 54, 55, 56,
    57, 82, 97, 154
stars, 65, 67, 74, 75, 84, 131
streets of gold, 1, 86, 91, 153

T

Tartarus, 32, 33, 42, 48, 57, 58, 61
temple, 87, 129, 148, 149, 150
Tetzel, Johann, 100
thief, 2, 95, 146, 147
Thomas, 69, 137

translation, 32, 33, 34, 41, 42, 44, 49, 56, 69, 95
tree of life, 92, 96
Tyre, 41

Z

Zion, 93, 94

Made in the USA
Middletown, DE
19 March 2015